WADSWORTH PHILOSOPHERS SERIES

ON

BUBER

C. Wayne Mayhall
University of Wales

Timothy B. Mayhall
Beeson Divinity School

THOMSON

WADSWORTH

Australia • Canada • Mexico • Singapore • Spain • United Kingdom • United States

Printed in Canada
1 2 3 4 5 6 7 07 06 05 04 03

Printer: Transcontinental-Louiseville

ISBN: 0-534-25232-X

For more information about our products, contact us at:
Thomson Learning Academic Resource Center
1-800-423-0563

For permission to use material from this text, contact us by:
Phone: 1-800-730-2214
Fax: 1-800-731-2215
Web: www.thomsonrights.com

For more information contact:
Wadsworth-Thomson Learning
10 Davis Drive
Belmont, CA 94002-3098
USA

Asia
Thomson Learning
5 Shenton Way #01-01
UIC Building
Singapore 068808

Australia/New Zealand
Thomson Learning
102 Dodds Street
Southbank, Victoria 3006
Australia

Canada
Nelson
1120 Birchmount Road
Toronto, Ontario M1K 5G4
Canada

Europe/Middle East/South Africa
Thomson Learning
High Holborn House
50-51 Bedford Row
London WC1R 4LR
United Kingdom

Latin America
Thomson Learning
Seneca, 53
Colonia Polanco
11560 Mexico D.F.
Mexico

Spain/Portugal
Paraninfo Thomson Learning
Calle/Magallanes, 25
28015 Madrid, Spain

For Payton Leyden (1989 – 2001)

Existence will remain meaningless for you if you yourself do not penetrate into it with your active love and if you do not in this way discover its meaning for yourself. Everything is waiting to be hallowed by you; it is waiting to be disclosed in its meaning and to be realized in it by you. He who loves brings God and the world together.

---Martin Buber, *The Way of Response*

Contents

Acknowledgments

We would like to acknowledge the kind readiness of Dr. Daniel Kolak, editor of the *Wadsworth Philosophers Series*. We would also like to thank our wives, Tamara and Laura, for their patience and encouragement during the writing of this monograph. We dedicate this book to Mordecai Martin Buber (1878 – 1965) whose writings, in the words of the critic G. S. Spinka, "are like cinnamon and phenolbarbitone – taken in small doses [they are] at one time stimulating and at another sobering." It is our hope that *On Buber,* in this small dose, will both "stimulate" and "sober" the serious reader in his or her present situation. Perhaps, in the process of becoming aware, the reader will begin to trace – with passion and precision – a path of response toward a global community built up out of mutual living relationships.

Preface

On Buber is an introduction to the most widely read Jewish thinker of our time, best known for his philosophy of dialogue. A volume in the *Wadsworth Philosophers Series*, it is a concise yet comprehensive engagement with Buber's most important ideas.

This volume, like the others in the series, is valuable in a number of ways. Serving as a stand-alone text when tackling Buber's original writings and as a helpful resource for focusing philosophy students' engagement with his often daunting concepts, it is also written for a popular readership in search of a clear overview to achieve quick familiarity with the great thinker's most lasting philosophical contributions.

Our aim is to initiate an introduction between the reader as individual and the man Martin Buber, too. In any introductory work there is an element of anxiety inherent in such a task quite often attributed to space restrictions. Restrictions aside, however, and regardless of how one chooses to relate to him – as a philosophical anthropologist, Jewish existentialist, poet-storyteller, or psychologist – there is the real possibility one may not truly come to know Buber without having spent much time in the company of his writings; an initiation which would need to include the integration of Buber's practical philosophy into one's own life experience.

In writing this introduction, we attempt to assist the reader in avoiding this anxiety. In the course of its unfolding, from the Overture to the Epilogue and all chapters in-between, this monograph attempts to preserve Buber's own self-revelation without unnecessary and excessive critical comment. We believe this is precisely how he would have wanted it. For Buber, self-revelation is a very personal matter. Self-revelation is the pathway to honest dialogue.

In his *Real Life Is Meeting*, the philosopher J.H. Oldham once wrote regarding Buber's classic *I and Thou,* "I question whether any book has been published in the present century the message of which, if it were understood, would have such far-reaching consequences for the life of our time." The reader and Buber must wrestle with "such far-reaching consequences." The writers take credit only for the introduction of two potential friends and hope such a poignant message may be understood between them.

The following abbreviations for Buber's works are used throughout this monograph: MB, *Martin Buber, Jewish Existentialist*; BM, *Between Man and Man*; D, *Daniel*; IT, *I and Thou*; EG, *Eclipse of God*; WR, *The Way of Response*; J, *On Judaism*; TF, *Two Types of Faith*; HM, *Hasidism and the Modern Man*. These citations appear initially in each chapter followed by the page number (i.e., BM, 109), and in subsequent references with page number only.

1
Overture

According to Martin Buber, when a person thinks, a person thinks with the entire body. The spiritual person thinks even with the fingertips. That we as a society can no longer carry on authentic dialogue one with another, he believes, is not only the most acute symptom of our pathological behavior, it is also a revelation that we have failed to realize exactly what is meant by his idea of "thinking." He writes of his philosophy's unique approach:

> I have occasionally described my standpoint to my friends as the "narrow ridge." I wanted by this to express that I did not rest on the broad upland of a system that includes a series of sure statements about the absolute, but on a narrow rocky ridge between the gulfs where there is no sureness of expressible knowledge but the certainty of meeting with the One who remains undisclosed (WR, 110).

As an *apertura* (overture), a first offering from this eminent thinker, and to set the tone for the remainder of our introductory journey along this "narrow rocky ridge between the gulfs," we join Buber in the midst of one of his own life experiences:

> On three successive evenings I spoke at the adult folk-school of a German industrial city on the subject "Religion as Reality." What I meant by that was the simple thesis that "faith" is not a feeling in the soul of man but an entrance into reality, an entrance into the *whole* reality without reduction and curtailment. This thesis is simple but it contradicts the usual way of thinking (EG, 3).

Buber needed three evenings, three lectures, and three discussions following the lectures to bring the audience to a point of understanding. As he progressed an uncomfortable silence among the workers in the crowd began to bother him, a silence not shared by the students and

1

other circles represented there. It was only at the end of the last evening that he had this silence explained to him.

One of the younger workers approached him: "Do you know, we can't speak in there, but if you would meet with us tomorrow, we could talk together the whole time." Buber agreed to meet with the small group on the following day, a Sunday. He writes:

> After dinner I came to the agreed place and now we talked together well into the evening. Among the workers was one, a man no longer young, whom I was drawn to look at again and again because he listened as one who really wished to hear. Real listening has become rare in our time. It is found most often among workers, who are not indeed concerned about the person speaking, as is so often the case with the *bourgeois* public, but about what he has to say (3).

The man, whose "curious face" reminded Buber of "an old Flemish altar picture representing the adoration of the shepherds one of them, who stretches out his arms toward the manger," sat before him listening with great intensity but without speaking a word of comment. Finally, however, he was moved to speak.

"I have had the experience," he explained slowly and impressively, Buber recalls, repeating a saying which the astronomer Laplace used in conversation with Napoleon, "that I do not need this hypothesis 'God' in order to be quite at home in the world (4)."

Buber was taken back by this brief yet curious proposal:

> I felt myself more deeply challenged than by the others. Up till then we had certainly debated very seriously, but in a somewhat relaxed way; now everything had suddenly become severe and hard. How should I reply to the man? I pondered awhile in the now severe atmosphere. It came to me that I must shatter the security of his *Weltanschauung*, through which he thought of a "world" in which one "felt at home."

The German terminology for a comprehensive philosophical view of the world and a person's place in it, this man's *Weltanschaung* deserved to be challenged, Buber decided. It begged the popular question about the type of world it was in which we live. It assumed that it is a world interpreted by and through sensory experience where "there exists vermilion and grass green, C major and B minor, [and] the taste of apple and of wormwood (4)." It seemed to ignore the possibility of perceiving the world as "anything other than the meeting of our own senses with those unapproachable events about whose essential definition physics always troubles itself in vain (4)." What of the world and its security? How to explain "phenomena" in light of the collision of unknown "objects" and well-known but not necessarily graspable "subjects?" Are these not three separate concepts difficult to bring together despite serious efforts to do so? Furthermore, what is the very essence of the foundation of this word's existence? Is there someone or something behind it all?

Buber continued to ask such troubling questions of the man, until it seemed he had asked enough:

> When I was through a stern silence ruled in the now twilit room. Then the man with the shepherd's face raised his heavy lids, which had been lowered the whole time, and said slowly and impressively, "You are right." I sat in front of him dismayed. What had I done? I had led the man to the threshold beyond which there sat enthroned the majestic image which the great physicist, the great man of faith, Pascal, called the God of the Philosophers. Had I wished for that? Had I not rather wished to lead him to the other, Him whom Pascal called the God of Abraham, Isaac, and Jacob. Him to whom one can say Thou (4)?

Dusk had settled in outside the meeting place and the evening grew long. Buber remembered that the following day he would have to depart, although he felt the conversation at a deadlock and the urge to remain engaged:

> I could not enter into the factory where the man worked, become his comrade, live with him, win his trust through real life-relationship, help him to walk with me the way of the creature who *accepts* the creation. I could only return his gaze (4).

In such a way, then, the conversation came to a close. In such a way, two men encountered life's deepest sentiments seemingly without resolve, yet not without experiencing the authenticity created by the depth of dialogue between them.

3

2
The Life of Dialogue

The Horse

At 69 years of age, with all of his usual extraordinary acuteness, Martin Buber writes of a decisive boyhood experience. In this moment he appears to suddenly realize the basic movement of the life of monologue, of one withdrawing one's true self from the world. This unfortunate withdrawal is not understood, he argues, in grasping the dichotomy which exists between the two possibilities of "turning away from" or "turning towards" someone. The move away from a real life of dialogue with others and towards a dialogue of fiction he calls *reflexion.*

Buber relates the story:

> When I was eleven years of age, spending the summer on my grandparents' estate, I used, as often as I could do it unobserved, to steal into the stable and gently stroke the neck of my darling, a broad dapple-grey horse. It was not a casual delight but a great, certainly friendly, but also deeply stirring happening.
>
> If I am to explain it now, beginning from the still very fresh memory of my hand, I must say that what I experienced in touch with the animal was the Other, the immense otherness of the Other, which, however, did not remain strange like the otherness of the ox and the ram, but rather let me draw near and touch it.
>
> When I stroked the mighty mane, sometimes marvelously smooth-combed, at other times just as astonishingly wild, and felt the life beneath my hand, it was as though the element of vitality itself bordered on my skin, something that was not I, was certainly not akin to me, palpably the other, not just another, really the Other itself; and yet it let me approach, confided itself to me,

4

placed itself elementally in the relation of *Thou* and *Thou* with me.

The horse, even when I had not begun by pouring oats for him into the manger, very gently raised his massive head, ears flicking, then snorted quietly, as a conspirator gives a signal meant to be recognizable only by his fellow-conspirator; and I was approved.

But once – I do not know what came over the child, at any rate it was childlike enough – it struck me about the stroking, what fun it gave me, and suddenly I became conscious of my hand. The game went on as before, but something had changed, it was no longer the same thing. And the next day, after giving him a rich feed, when I stroked my friend's head he did not raise his head.

A few years later, when I thought back to the incident, I no longer supposed that the animal had noticed my defection. But at the time I considered myself judged (BM, 22-3).

For Buber *reflexion* is a habit more dangerous than egotism and nothing less than the source of the disintegration of the mysterious reality of true intercourse between two human worlds.

Reflexion is not about the person concerned with the Other. It is the woman who pauses with her essential being – like the young Buber before the powerful horse – before another person and lets the Other exist only as an extension of her own experience; merely as a part of herself.

The man who fears to plunge into the silent unity which exists when two individuals come together, but instead imposes upon the moment a judgment upon the other experiences *reflexion*.

Encountering Buber

Experiencing Martin Buber is like entering through a single door opening to you. Walk in through the door and you are suddenly faced with many closed doors. In order to find the way out of this existential sphere he creates you will need to begin opening each door. But to do so is to confront yet another revelation of purpose:

There is a purpose to creation; there is a purpose to the human race, one we have not made up ourselves, or agreed to among ourselves; we have not decided that henceforward this, that, or the other shall serve as the purpose of our existence. No. The purpose itself revealed its face to us and we have gazed upon it (WR, 130).

In the vignette above, for example, as we step through the door of "reflexion" via the sensory experiences of a young boy, the purpose revealed in this encounter might shock us into questioning how we interact with others whom we know. In the curious face of the man "no longer young" or the wondering hand of the precocious eleven-year-old on the mane of the dapple-grey horse, we become privy to the seeds of contemplation sown in the heart and mind through human experience.

Buber is widely recognized as one of the leading religious thinkers of our time and his writing compares to a well-rehearsed symphony of interdisciplinary fields harmonizing, without one particular discipline taking first chair. To read *I and Thou* or the *Eclipse of God*, for example, is to be exposed to current philosophical, theological, and sociological theories on the matter of "being" – what will be referred to as "ontology" here forward.

It has been suggested that the best way to come to an understanding of Buber's place in the world of other thinkers is simply to watch him interact in a group environment where his peers are bombarding him with questions about what it is he believes about a particular subject.

One of the most frequently asked questions of Buber is put forth to challenge his *I-Thou* philosophy especially as it regards an apparent idealist trend toward what is known as "panpsychism." From the Greek "pan" meaning all and "psyche" meaning soul or mind, panpsychism is the view according to which a mental element is present in everything that exists from animate to inanimate objects. The term is often associated with the view known as "immaterialism," which is the idea that matter doesn't really exist and there are no material objects. The very act of existence, to exist as a being *qua* (as) being is a matter of perception or of being perceived by or with a mind.

The question might be put to Buber as such: "When a person goes out into nature and encounters the tree, is it possible in such an encounter for the I-Thou relationship to be established?" Instead of directly answering the question (anticipating the accusation which might follow), Buber answers with a question of his own. Paraphrased roughly, he asks, "Have you yourself ever had an experience, such as coming around the bend of a winding mountain road, where you were compelled to pull to the side to take in the view of the awe-inspiring valley thousands of feet beneath your feet?" At this point, each participant in the dialogue disarmed, the real conversation begins.

Early Years

Born on February 8, 1878, in Vienna, Austria, Buber is only three years of age when his mother abandons he and his father for a different life and marriage in Russia. The disappearance means a move from the city of Vienna to the city of Lvov (Lemberg), Galacia, and to the spacious estate of Solomon and Adele Wizer-Buber.

A remarkable and eccentric man, Solomon is an esteemed rabbinic scholar. He is also a successful entrepreneur who had found a prosperous life in the business of agriculture, especially farming. Adele, too, is remarkably well-educated, a woman "who was one of those Jewesses of that period who, in order to create freedom and leisure for their husbands to study the Torah, managed their businesses for them." Growing up on his grandparents estate, Buber is exposed to an exemplary education:

In his household the young grandson experienced the harmonious union of the authentic Jewish tradition with the liberating spirit of the Enlightenment or Haskalah. In particular he imbibed the atmosphere of healthy piety and profound respect for learning which were to set the framework for his whole life. Jewish tradition, Jewish learning, the study of the Bible and of classical Hebrew, both written and spoken, provided the permanent basis for his life.

At age 14, however, Buber rejoins his father, who has now re-married and he is enrolled in the Polish grammar school in Lemberg. Of his father he writes:

[He] took part in the life of all the people who were in one way or another dependent on him – the laborers...the peasants...the tenants. He concerned himself with their family lives, with the upbringing of and schooling of the children...This solicitude was not derived from any principles but was directly personal. This same way of acting in relationship to people carried over into the town. 'He understood no other help than that from person to person'.

Carl Buber's influence on the young Martin's life would not be of a particularly intellectual impact, but a son would come to appreciate a father's role as the instructor of the more practical and relational aspects of society, which he would one day thoroughly explore in intimate detail.

"Thus Spoke..." Kant and Nietzsche

Before his time at the grammar school is over, the young Buber completely immerses himself in the study of languages and the humanities, and is very much an expert on the philosophies of Immanuel Kant and of Fredrich Nietzsche. From Kant he learns of a crucial distinction between philosophy in the scholastic sense and philosophy in the universal sense. True philosophy should move beyond the simple academic exercise of history and into life application; answers to the essential questions of being should translate into more meaningful interpersonal relationships. Buber discovers the roots of philosophical anthropology in four questions put forth by Kant: *What can I know?*; *What ought I to do?*; *What may I hope?*; *What is man?*. Metaphysics answers the first question, ethics the second, religion the third, and anthropology the fourth.

It is in these formative years, too, that Buber attempts to translate Nietzsche's *Thus Spake Zarathustra* into Polish. He is influenced, as are most philosophically minded sorts during this time, by the unorthodox and penetrating thought and writing style of the philosopher. The young Buber is inspired by Nietzsche's philosophy of summoning the power of the human will to transcend the hypocritical religious fetters binding the individual to illusion for a life which creates the real future person who can overcome the present weaker version. At some point he is recorded to have said, "We do not will a revolution. We are a revolution."

Zioinism

In the autumn of 1896 Buber begins studies at the University of Vienna and immediately devotes himself to the study of the humanities such as philosophy and cultural studies and lays aside a once anticipated involvement in his Jewish history. Like many of the cities of Europe, Vienna is experiencing the crest of a "Golden Age" at the closing of the 19th century. It is a romantic time fueled by a renaissance in the arts and empirical sciences. Yet, despite its strong influence on Buber, the cultural extremes soon become a source of irritation to him and his experiences at the university become merely fodder for his philosophical scrapbook.

It is a movement known as Zionism which immediately engrosses Buber the student, and in 1901 he becomes the editor of the movement's mouthpiece, the journal *Die Welt*. The term Zionism was coined in 1893 by Nathan Birnbaum (1864-1937), an early proponent of this national movement for the return of the Jewish people to their homeland and the resumption of Jewish sovereignty in Israel. From its inception Zionism advocated both tangible and spiritual aims and was embraced by Jews of all persuasions, left and right, religious and secular.

Although his time with the journal is brief due to irreconcilable differences between he and another leader in the Zionist movement, Buber is captivated by his involvement on the radical edge of an idea which seems to have such immediate far-reaching sociological impact. Within months he relocates to Berlin and establishes with a few friends his own Jewish publishing company, the *Judische Verlag*, which quickly receives notice throughout all of central Europe for its frontline publications.

In brief, Buber embraces Zionism because it is a proper corrective for certain trends in the Jewish tradition which have resulted in a moving away from the foundational creeds which historically define his people – trends such as capitalistic enterprising and the resultant commercialization of Jewish culture.

Hasidism

Buber's complete immersion in the Zionist movement and his withdrawal from the secular university environment reach a point where the young activist finds himself disconcerted with the frantic pace of his life, even to the point of questioning exactly what it is he is trying to accomplish. This withdrawal results in his giving up a highly public profile among the Jewish community and results in a self-imposed isolation. He becomes deeply involved in the study of the texts and traditions of Hasidism.

Hasidism (HAH-see-DIZZ-um), is a form of mystical Orthodox Judaism that began in the 1700's in Eastern Europe. It was founded by Rabbi Israel ben Eliezer, who is better known as the Baal Shem Tov (Besht for short) which means *Master of the Good Name* in Hebrew. This solitary time, from 1904 to 1909, will eventually have far-reaching consequences on the rest of Buber's life and work. In Hasidism, Buber writes, "I recognized the idea of the complete man. At the same time I became conscious of the call to make this known to the world."

Kierkegaard

After the solitary years of studying Hasidism, Buber encounters the writings of the Danish existentialist Soren Kierkegaard (1813-1855) which have been translated from Danish into German. Kierkegaard's philosophy centers around the concept that the passions which shape a person's being are "inwardness" and "subjectivity," two ideas which have come to be the cornerstone of what is known today as the philosophy of existentialism. Existentialism, among its many other various levels of definition, is at its core a focus on the uniqueness of each human individual as opposed to the individual as part of a system of abstract human qualities.

A person becomes a true "subjective" self through a "leap" from the world of useless intellectual reflection (recall Buber's "reflexion") toward the third and final stage of realization that life has to offer. Kierkegaard's first "stage on life's way," is that of the *aesthetic life* lived in the moment and dictated by a person satisfying a never-ending drone of insatiable desires. The aesthetic person lacks the commitment and discipline to live a life with meaning and purpose. The *ethical life* is the second stage and is marked by commitment to a life of meaning and value lacked by that of the aesthetic individual. This stage, however, lacks the understanding of the transcendent power inherent in true ideals which far outweighs those created to sustain the merely human sphere of activity. Were this realization of transcendence as immanence to occur, the individual would have made the leap into the *religious life,* the third and final stage on life's way, and into "eternal validitiy."

Kierkegaard, Hasidism and his passionate commitment to Jewish studies swirls together in the philosophical exploration of the young Buber. Although there are times when he finds himself strongly criticizing certain aspects of Kierkegaard's thought, he finds solace and inspiration in the similarities between Hasidism's philosophy of the individual's practical marriage of community and theology and Kierkegaard's practical marriage of the religious life and the ethical and aesthetic spheres. Both of these essential combinations, for Buber, work in tandem to strongly influence first the individual and secondly the society in which the individual lives and moves.

Academic

The year of the publication of his best known work, *I and Thou,* 1923 is also the year Buber takes his first professorship at Frankfurt University, Germany. His role as a teacher of Jewish History of Religion and Ethics is brought to an abrupt ending in 1933, however, with the rise of the German Socialist Party and the rule of the Nazis. He does not leave Germany – as many of his closest friends do either by force or because of fear – and from his home in Heppenheim, a small village on the river on the Bergstrasse, he continues to reach out to Jewish compatriots throughout all of Europe, offering them encouragement and support in a time of great struggle and disillusionment.

In 1938, at sixty years of age, Buber relocates to Palestine to teach sociology at the Hebrew University of Jerusalem. He has at last arrived at the place he always considered his true home and Buber quickly settles into a frenzy of political and intellectual output. Many of the editorial pieces he writes during this time concern the current affairs of his Jewish community worldwide, from the horrors of the Nazi regime visited upon them to the great injustices Buber believes are being visited upon the Jewish Nationals in the homeland by overtly anti-Semitic factions.

The Way of Response

Buber's writings span six decades and cover a multitude of interests ranging from the mystical nature of Hasidism to the practical applications of Zionism and philosophies as diverse and differentiated as existentialism and Marxism. If there is an attempt to find one motif which runs through each of the exploratory stages of his career, however, it would inevitably come down to a position best defined in the phrase he uses time and time again, "the way of response."

It has been said that, for Buber, it is through the other that I become fully I – an idea in opposition Nietzsche's dictum that one only experiences oneself in the end. It is in his own story of the conversion from the "religious" to the "possibility of dialogue" that we discover Buber the person behind the concept:

> In my earlier years the "religious" was for me the exception. There were hours that were taken out of the course of things. From somewhere or other the firm crust of everyday was pierced. Then the reliable permanence of appearances broke down; the attack which took place burst its law asunder. "Religious experience" was the experience of an otherness which did not fit into the context of life (WR, 17).

There is on one hand the mystical aspect of "religious experience" which transports a person from this world to an other-worldly state, where time is destroyed and rapture born. For Buber there is an inherent "illegitimacy" in this journey. This uncomfortable division becomes real to him through an everyday experience, what he calls "an event of judgment." It occurs in the afternoon, just after a morning of "religious" activity, when he receives a visit from an unknown man:

> ...without being there in spirit. I certainly did not fail to let the meeting be friendly, I did not treat him any more remissly than all his contemporaries who were in the habit of seeking me out about

12

this time of day as an oracle that is ready to listen to reason. I conversed attentively and openly with him – only I omitted to guess the questions which he did not put. Later, not long after, I learned from one of his friends – he himself was no longer alive – the essential content of these questions; I learned that he had come to me not casually, but borne out of destiny, not for a chat but for a decision. He had come to me, he had come in this hour. What do we expect when we are in despair and yet go to a man? Surely a presence by means of which we are told that nevertheless there is meaning (18).

When he comes to fully realize what he has, or in this case has not, done Buber abandons the so-called "religious," the idea of ecstasy or escape from the very real moments contained in each new day. There is now nothing left for him but the everyday, and he will dedicate himself to it:

The mystery is no longer disclosed, it has escaped or it has made its dwelling here where everything happens as it happens. I know no fullness but each mortal hour's fullness of claim and responsibility. Though far from being equal to it, yet I know that in the claim I am claimed and may respond in responsibility (18).

Buber is recognized as the quintessential philosopher in the world, experiencing life and, in turn, journaling these experiences in such a personal way that all who come to encounter them will experience Buber, too, translating his world into their very own.

Malcolm L. Diamond, who translated several of Buber's works into English, recalls a story Buber once told him, which captures Buber's unique response to life in its finest nuance:

He had just returned from a visit to the United States of America, and was full of his impressions. He told me a little story of his journey across New York City in a taxi-cab. The driver was talkative, and the following dialogue ensued:

Driver: I have been reading an article by a strange fellow. He says that you shouldn't be angry, but should solve your

13

differences by being patient and seeking peace with the other person.

Buber: I agree.

Driver: He was a strange man, 700 years old.

Buber: A great age.

Driver: Yes. His name was Francis.

Buber: I know him too. I can tell you a lot of stories about him.

So they talked of Francis, and finally Buber was deposited at the book-store he wished to visit. The driver departed, and some time later, when the taxi was long gone, Buber noticed that he had lost his spectacle-case. Before he had time to do anything about it, the driver reappeared, spectacle-case in hand. 'Good boy,' said Buber; and before all the people the driver leant his head for a moment on Buber's shoulder, and thus they embraced.

Buber believes wholeheartedly that the life between birth and death, in all its fragility, can nevertheless be worthwhile if only there is dialogue and persons are courageous enough to practice responsibility for their role in thought, speech and action. This fulfillment, however, is only really possible in the act of a confession of inadequacy on the individual's part.

3
Daniel

Why, when this span of life might be fleeted away
as laurel, a little darker than all
the surrounding green, with tiny waves on the border
of every leaf (like the smile of a wind): - oh, why
have to be human, and, shunning Destiny,
long for Destiny?...

---Rilke

English scholar J. B. Morse once wrote Buber to tell him of the influence his book *Daniel* (1913) had on the esteemed Austrian-born poet Maria Ranier Rilke (1875-1926). Intrigued by the introduction of the mystical philosophy of dialogue in this, Buber's earliest work, he appears to have considered its content in the writing of his *Ninth Duino Elegy*, as demonstrated in the verse above.

Considering the initial reception of *Daniel*, it is ironic that Buber refuses for many years the publication of an English translation of the work because he believes it does not reflect his mature thought, which is eventually revealed in his seminal work *I and Thou*, published a decade later in 1923. It isn't until 1964, fifty-one years after its initial German publication, that Buber consents to oversee the translation with the stipulation that the translator write a lengthy introduction "explaining, at some length, that [*Daniel*] is an early book in which there is already expressed the great duality of human life, but only in its cognitive and not yet in its communicative and existential character (D, *Preface*)."

Daniel represents Buber's transition to a radical new existential way of thinking and writing and is a passageway to his mature writings. In this work he is clearly struggling between the two poles of his early mystical background and his encounter with the philosophy of dialogue. He asks the question: how to reconcile the desire for community and relationship with the Other with one's own ontological insecurity?

Often a person is alone in a world of others; Buber knows this all too well from his own life experience. Confronting the risk to act and to

15

receive the actions of others, with all the unpredictable consequences involved, a person experiences uncertainty. Yet, if one chooses not to act non-action can result in a distance between oneself and others. One is left to reconcile this dilemma with the memory of those moments in life, when caught up in the rapture of fellowship with the Other and lost in the reverie of togetherness, action seemed worthwhile.

This either-or dilemma is for Buber the crux of his mature philosophy expressed in *I and Thou* which will concern us in the next chapter. The fleshing-out of the paradoxical unity of the life of dialogue and the desire for mystical union is not so apparent, however, in his earlier years.

The unique blend of conversations between Daniel and his companions in various settings allows the work to speak to the human condition described above in such a way as to foreshadow Buber's poetical philosophy developed in *I and Thou*. A work of fiction pulsing with philosophical and theological insight, *Daniel* is also a wonderfully well-written piece of literature which stands on its own, revealing the incredible sensitivity and insight the young Buber possesses.

Background

In his introduction to *Daniel*, translator Maurice Friedman writes:

Buber's concern for unity, realization, creativity, action, and form is expressed for the first time entirely in its own terms and not as the interpretation of some particular thought or religious or cultural movement. *Daniel* is the first mature and comprehensive expression of Buber's early philosophy, and it is at the same time the most creative and organically whole of his books to appear until that time. It shows the way in which Buber's philosophy has grown out of a number of the decisive experiences of his life, and its poetic and dialogical form gives us an important emotional insight into Buber's early thought (18).

In each of the five "Dialogues" Daniel is with a friend. In each dialogue, set in its own unique geographical backdrop, a question (or series of questions) is put forth between friends; the sort of questioning in which deep calls to deep, where philosophical inquiry delves into the core meaning of being and existence is summoned out of the shadows.

The first dialogue in the mountains attempts to come to terms with an understanding of power and direction. The second dialogue above the city speaks to a deeper understanding of reality. The third dialogue in the garden concerns itself with the meaning of this deeper reality. The fourth dialogue after Daniel and a friend have been to the theater moves toward an understanding of the polarity of unreality and reality. The fifth dialogue by the sea engages the idea of unity among disunity.

On Direction – "Dialogue in the Mountains"

In this first dialogue, Daniel and his partner (known only as "The Woman") are hiking a mountainous terrain. She poses a question:

> *The Woman*: Would we not be miserable – creatures flung into a stale existence – if we were not born again every morning out of the abyss of sleep?
> *Daniel*: Because we cannot circle above all existence – sleepless, unbroken, boundless, glowing – we content ourselves with being submerged and awakening. Because we cannot ascend into the spaceless...(50).

Awakening (direction) and *form* (space we occupy as opposed to "spaceless" or the unknown we can't) are two terms Buber continually explores. Each person will travel a unique path to understanding God. Along the way the individual is constantly confronted with the option to turn away in misdirection from the undisclosed mystery contained in each moment of the journey.

Power is the force behind direction. But power alone cannot illuminate the heart of experience, just as direction without power can supply only meaning without substance. It is the combination of both which allows a person to go beyond superficial encounter and into the substance and true reality of experience.

According to Buber, the person who is properly directed and who has a true sense of the necessary power proportionate to moving into community with others – without imposing over and against the Other – will experience growth in all areas of life, according to Buber.

Form must have this power and direction so that a person's life will possess stability and ontological security enough to make possible sustained existence in a society and a culture which assumes a foundation of personal integration and growth (enough to join in). Form represents the boundaries which direct the impulses of individuals but, unfortunately, in society the external patterns which make up these boundaries eventually double back on society, according to Buber, and distort the energy into a destructive force.

On Reality – "Dialogue Above the City"

Ulrich: *And perhaps it is this that allows us to feel our knowledge as something living and indestructible even when it is preserved in silence...But what was it, Daniel, that you knew at that time?*
Daniel: *If I may say it to you as simply as I knew it: he remains unreal who does not realize* (64).

What is it to realize, to relate the experiences of life with nothing but their distinct moments alone? If a person finds the answer to this question, a person is in a place where the spirit is awakened to become creative and unified in every act. To run from the chaos of experience and to refuse to bring direction and order to life is resigned laziness "which leaves the doors of the past open and turns to every shadow the same bittersweet attentiveness (68)," writes Buber:

> ...where orientation rules, that crafty economy is at home whose shrewdness stinks to heaven because it only saves and never renews. But where the foot of realization stands, there power is drawn from the depths and collected and moved to action and renewed in work (69).

"To realize," then, is to experience each moment as a moment in and of itself without judging it based on the past with its wounds or the future with its uncertainties. For Daniel, all of one's being must engage the single thing or event to actualize true reality.

The curse of orientation is the progress of science and the information overflow science creates. *Reification* (Latin – *res* "thing" and *facere* "to make"), is the error of treating as a "thing" something which is not one and is a result of this progress. The individual is ruled by the instruments designed to make appearance as imitation the backdrop of an impersonal world of unreality.

On Meaning – "Dialogue in the Garden"

Daniel: *And this is your nearest danger: descend into the abyss! Realize it! Know its nature, the thousand-named, nameless polarity of all being, between piece and piece of the world, between thing and thing, between image and being, between the world and you, in the very heart of yourself, at all places, with its swinging tensions and its streaming reciprocity* (98).

In the age of innocence, when all seemed simple and straightforward, Daniel's friend Reinold recalls, even worries were quickly classified and put under the rule of innocence. But in the age of innocence lost and in the endless search to recapture what once was, hopelessness is a mist which shrouds the depth of the abyss. Solitude and eternal distance from the world create a great chasm between thought and action, between true and false self.

Reinold speaks of his disillusionment with the "world-knowers," "God-knowers," "mind-knowers," and the "knowers of mystery." The world-knowers embrace the abyss between things and consciousness, denying a connection between objects of observation and ideas of reality existing beyond the sensory world. The God-knowers embrace the abyss between man and God, denying the person can conceive of an absolute beyond her own thinking self. The mind-knowers embrace the abyss between the idea and the experience and like the world-knowers believe the mind is all there is and thought is the master of the moment. The knowers of mystery embrace the abyss between the world of appearance and the true world, remaining so heavenly-minded earthly reality is of no consequence.

It is a dangerous thing to live with one's entire being. There is the abyss if genuine knowledge sacrifices itself for a form of Truth consisting of having knowledge and not becoming known to others. Security is the watchword for the orienting person and orientation which seeks a totalizing theory of all people and all things must inevitably embrace a world without God.

On the other hand, the realizing person possesses direction and meaning in such a way as to award his very being with a true freedom. He is able to realize himself in reality and to relate himself to each single moment and to the intrinsic value contained within the moment without shouldering the burden of unnecessary paranoia – which might otherwise accompany the orienting person in search of security.

On Polarity – "Dialogue After the Theater"

Leonhard: *Did the play move you so, Daniel? As you walk next to me, imprisoned in silence, it feels to me as if we did not come the same way...*

Daniel: *I come from the theater, Leonhard, and what has moved me and set me into a silence is the theater itself. I saw it today for the first time* (101).

Daniel observes in the play for the first time the meaninglessness of duality, not the duality which exists between the problem of good and evil, but that which exists in the struggle of a person coming to terms with what it means to be or not to be, the duality between being and counter-being:

> I found *myself* over against that other being who moved on the state and conversed with himself. For without its weakening its inner cleavage, indeed at the very time when it had become more lively and stood more in relief…it stood over against my We-I, as the storm the stillness…(107)

The relation between "I" and "Thou" which is developed in the next chapter is the culmination of this polarity which Daniel struggles to explain. There is a given misunderstanding which leads to common confusion between individuals attempting to relate to one another on a meaningful level. This misunderstanding is the tension driving all dialogue toward either positive or negative poles and it is the revelation Daniel attempts to understand after the final curtain falls upon the actors and their words.

In the proceeding dialogues Daniel experiences, the overwhelming subject of study is that of the unity of the individual with nature, the other, others, and transcendent reality. In this dialogue, however, the emphasis is obviously on the concept of being-over-against other being and the haunting awareness that no bridge exists, despite all human effort to close the existential gap.

On Unity – "Dialogue by the Sea"

Daniel: *We spoke of death, my friend Lukas; we have all the time spoken of nothing else. You wish to know the holy sea, the unity that bears life and death in right and left hand. You cannot know it otherwise than when you take upon yourself the tension of life and death and live through the life and death of the world as your life and your death. Then the I of this tension will awaken in you – the unconditioned, the unity of life and death* (144).

None of the ways in which the wisdom of the ages attempts to understand true unity of person can satisfy Daniel, he concludes in the fifth and final "Dialogue by the Sea." In order to find himself and the "mystery of life-experience" he realizes he is going to have to forsake all the inadequate ways wisdom has put before him.

One wrong way is to create an illusory path where one convinces himself that there is no duality in the world. It is easy to create in the mind of the single individual a world without trouble or disunity. Yet, in order utopia, one must remove himself from the cruel edges of society where the reality between good and evil is revealed in the streets – at any given moment, perhaps…around the next corner.

A second way of escape from the duality offered by worldly wisdom, which appears wrong to Daniel, is the attempt to think this duality together with unity. This is the futile attempt by the individual to accept an identity at the edge of the abyss which refuses to look down into the darkness below for fear of becoming disoriented. It is a fact of life, however, that in order to truly understand reality a descent into the abyss on "the clattering highway on which I live" will be essential.

All of Daniel's dialogues culminate in this last dialogue. Its focus on death. A realization of life in the midst of death is for Buber the best example to bring Daniel and his friends in dialogue to a place of accepting reality in its unpredictable flow. The sea as a symbol of infinity and transcendence beyond life's duality is present in a variety of dialogical situations in *Daniel*. In its stillness and depth it reflects the face of man back to him and the backdrop of creation behind him. Both absorb him into its depths in an act of disappearing from the world and expels him from its depths in an act of seeing the world for the first time. In its violence, however, the sea engulfs the vessel created by the hands of man and swallows him up in chaos before silencing him forever.

A year ago, Lukas shares with Daniel that his friend was drowned at sea at this very place. For Lukas there is an acute awareness of having transferred his own existential struggle onto his friend during that fateful day of reckoning. Every morning he imagines himself sailing the boat; the demon of life sitting at the rudder and the goddess of death in the prow.

Lukas asks the question of his experience whose answer never comes to comfort him. Why is this sea so much like the life which appears to contain the very secret of life and death upon its surface?

"The sum of life is the sum of its unconditionedness," Daniel tells him. "The might of a life is the might of its unity. He who dies in the completed unity of his life utters the I that is not inserted, that is the naked eternity (143-44)." The faithful individual, Daniel shares with Lukas, is the person who lives in and through the often unpredictable duality of life, "who receives and endures its fearful blessings." The

21

faithful individual no longer fears moving beyond the illusions once needed to sustain the security required to avoid this duality. As a diver plunges to the bottom of the sea to measure its mysterious depths, the person of faith embraces the life's whirlwind of division and contradiction to bring about unity among disunity.

4

I and Thou

So, waiting, I have won from you the end: God's presence in each element.

---Goethe

Ich und Du (*I and Thou*), first appeared in the German edition in 1923, and in the English translation in 1937. Buber's most widely circulated philosophical treatise, *I and Thou* focuses on what makes an authentic conversation or relationship. Buber's emphasis on the concept of dialogue first introduced in *Daniel* reaches maturity and is defined in this work as a conversation or a relationship that involves the concrete circumstances of the participants and assumes the presence of God as the foundation of such a relation. It also assumes that such an encounter escapes the disintegration of the world built around and depending on the *It* of objectification of person, place or thing.

Buber introduces *I and Thou* with a description of man's twofold attitude:

> To man the world is twofold, in accordance with his twofold attitude. The attitude of man is twofold, in accordance with the twofold nature of the primary words which he speaks. The primary words are not isolated words, but combined words. The one primary word is the combination *I-Thou*. The other primary word is the combination *I-It*; wherein, without a change in the primary word, one of the words *He* and *She* can replace *It*. Hence the *I* of man is also twofold. For the *I* of the primary word *I-Thou* is a different *I* from that of the primary word *I-It* (IT, 3).

The primary word combinations are *I-Thou* and *I-It* (or *I-He*, *I-She*). These primary words do not represent things but relationships between things and people and between things, people and the *Thou*. In Buber's writings the *Thou* clearly represents the personal God of the Judeo-Christian tradition with his particularly unique characterization of this God based on Jewish mystical and Hasidic teachings.

23

The *I* of *I-Thou* is not separable from the *Thou* to which it addresses nor is the *I* of *I-It* separable from the *It* in the process of being spoken and understood. Both relationships concern, ultimately, the ontological status of relationship as it stands between one person and another, a person and an object or a person and God. In turn all of the relationships as they represent individuals naturally translate into society to represent the attitudes and orientation of the people who collectively create culture. The concept of *I-Thou* is for Buber the quintessential orientation spoken by a person with the entire being whereas *I-It* speaks of the relationship of the person who is incomplete and cannot speak from the ground of being.

There are three parts to *I and Thou*. In Part One Buber parses out the primary terms he first introduces, separating them in such a way as to represent the different spheres of reality explored a decade earlier in *Daniel* – those of destiny, reality, experiencing, using, form, and continuity. There is a brief history of primal man's interaction with objects and others and a definition in broad strokes of how the *Thou* has always been the over-arching theme pressing a people toward a relationship of spirit and soul stretching beyond that of object and form. Part Two is Buber stretching the definition of the *I-It* relationship and the overall effect such a relationship has on personal growth toward freedom of spirit and destiny. In Part Three the characteristics and results of a proper relationship exclusively with the *Thou* are presented in example and story in such a manner as to move the reader toward silence and meditation upon the revelation of the *Thou*.

The Spheres of Relation

There are three spheres of relation within the world. The first sphere, *our life with nature*, contains the relationship of person to creature which oral communication cannot penetrate. Certainly it is possible to tell the pet to fetch or sit, but no one would claim that the pet actually understands what it means to "fetch" or to "sit." It is simply responding instinctually to the inseparable relationship between the measured sound of the delivery of the word and the immediate motion its body has been trained to exhibit, so that one could easily say "sit" and expect the pet to run off after a tennis ball if that is what the body associates with the word "sit" and an object being thrown. In the second sphere, *our life with men*, on the other hand, relationship is established through speech and the more the words exchanged or understood in terms of concepts which translate into meaning the richer the relationship between the two people can be. It is in this sphere, too,

Buber believes we are able to give to another and to accept from others the *Thou*. Exactly how this works is not clear at this point. In the third sphere, *our life with spiritual beings*, we engage the *Thou* in all of its mystical transcendence. The *Thou* does not speak with the apparatus (lungs inhale, vocal chords vibrate, tongue and mouth move) of the human being yet is the very author of human speech:

> We perceive no *Thou*, but nonetheless we feel we are addressed and we answer – forming, thinking, acting. We speak the primary word with our being, though we cannot utter *Thou* with our lips (6).

In each of the three spheres and in each of the processes of becoming we experience there is the experience of being addressed by and in turn addressing the eternal Thou, writes Buber, but this occurs only if we are open to such a possibility.

Poems and songs have been written about the loveliness and the majesty of a tree, but before Buber, no philosopher had ever considered in such unique fashion objects of root, bark and leaf in order to explain the meaning of belonging to the spheres of relation.

A person can see the tree in a photograph or a picture, or see it in the front yard tossed about by the wind and realize that underneath its inanimate exterior there is a world of movement taking place: water taken in from the roots moving up into the trunk and flowing out into the tiny leaves attached to its branches; photosynthesis; a tap for maple syrup; these are but a few of its many ways it marks its "ceaseless commerce with earth and air." The tree can be classified and studied, cut down or taken up and replanted somewhere else, but regardless, in all of these the tree is still an object to the *I* manipulating it.

There is a way of looking at the tree, however, in which the *I* can become "bound up in relation to it" to the point that the tree is "no longer *It*," and the *I* is "seized by the power of exclusiveness." It is simply a matter of ceasing to classify the tree into its separate functions or considering it as an image on photographic paper or an object to be manipulated for personal satisfaction, although considering all of these aspects of relation to the tree do not have to be given up. Instead, the *I* simply stops imagining the tree as consisting of all these separate categories in and of itself and encounters the tree for the first time, not as "soul or dryad" but as a tree, "the tree itself."

It is the same to face another human being, writes Buber:

...he is not a thing among things and does not consist of things. Thus human being is not He or She, bounded from every other He and She, a specific point in space and time within the net of the world; nor is he a nature able to be experienced and described, a loose bundle of named qualities. But with no neighbour, and whole in himself, he is *Thou* and fills the heavens. This does not mean that nothing exists except himself. But all else lives in his light (8).

The melody is not the notes, the verse is not the words or sentences, prayer is not about time, sacrifice is not about the space in which to do it; although, notes proceed before the melody, words and sentences the verse, time must make room for prayer and space for sacrifice. So it is with the person addressed as *Thou*. *I* cannot experience the person addressed as *Thou* in terms of an act of experience. Only when *I* relates to *Thou* ceasing to analyze the experience of relating itself does *I* come close to *Thou*. "In the act of experience," writes Buber, "*Thou* is far away (9)."

Direct and Indirect Relation

It is a given expectation among those who teach its content, who have read and re-read *I and Thou* – and who attempt to integrate Buber's "new epistemology" into the historical background of philosophy and theology – that the first-time reader will inevitably succumb to the temptation toward frustration with the back and forth. Buber's explaining the differences between the *Thou* and the *It* and the relationship each of these has with the *I* can quickly become entwined so that the purpose of finding existential meaning truth takes a back seat to sorting out which is which.

Aware, however, of exactly what Buber is aware as he weaves each section of the work together to create the rich tapestry of its 120 pages, the wise mentor is content to deliver *I and Thou* into the hands of the reader without commentary, only anticipating there will occur a meeting between its cryptic message and the mind trained to follow logic and structure at a point further into its depths.

When Buber asks, "What, then, do we experience of *Thou*?," and answers, "Just nothing. For we do not experience it," the basic linguistic logic of language dictates that the *Thou* cannot be known or experienced. Therefore, it can be assumed the *Thou* is not an object to be apprehended by the senses and in such an observation, from the point of view of the person who believes only in what can be classified and analyzed, this *Thou* is nothing but a meaningless word. But when Buber follows this question with the question, "What, then, do we know of *Thou*?," and answers, "Just everything. For we know nothing isolated about it any more," there is an apparent contradiction. Do we know nothing or everything about the *Thou*? Or perhaps we know everything there is to know which is exactly that there is nothing to know about the *Thou*? If this is so, then we are back at square one. The *Thou* represents nothing and is meaningless. Or is it?

Philosophers have long identified various ways of knowing something to be true and have done so in such detail and content that their activity warrants its own field of study known as epistemology (Greek: *episteme*, "knowledge," and *logos*, "explanation"). Epistemology is concerned with the nature of knowledge and with how something known is justified as being true or false.

The above dilemma concerns two different sorts of knowledge in collision with one another. One of these is known as propositional knowledge (the *Thou* is either nothing or the *Thou* is everything), while the other is non-propositional knowledge, that is acquired through a direct awareness or acquaintance with something (e.g., the *Thou* is both nothing and something and this is verified not by logic but by direct relationship). The former is empirical knowledge (a posteriori – following after) which occurs through verification of sensory experience and the latter is non-empirical (a priori – prior to) knowledge which comes through innate or inherent knowledge.

Buber is at best arguing for an a priori, non-empirical, non-propositional knowledge of the *I-Thou* relationship He argues for this in such a way that such a knowledge base is constructed in a congenial epistemic environment and the person acquiring this knowledge is in his or her right mind. Therefore, this knowing of the *Thou* and subsequent relationship with the *Thou* is in itself propositional, empirical and a posteriori to sensory experience with the *Thou* and others:

> The *Thou* meets me through grace – it is not found by seeking. The *Thou* meets me. But I step into direct relation with it...All real living is meeting...The relation to the *Thou* is direct (11).

There is "no system of ideas, no foreknowledge, and no fancy" to intervene between the relating of the *I* and *Thou*, according to Buber. But is he saying that knowledge of the *Thou* is outside of all we know through the idea, or a presupposition of knowledge which comes through sensory experience? He answers the question:

> The memory is transformed, as it plunges out of its isolation into the unity of the whole. No aim, no lust, and no anticipation intervene between *I* and *Thou*. Desire itself is transformed as it plunges out of its dream into the appearance. Every means is an obstacle. Only when every means has collapsed does the meeting come about (12).

Relating between the *I* and the *Thou* creates a real presence in the real world that makes the reality which precedes it irrelevant and illusory. When the *I* encounters the *Thou* in this place true being is lived, whereas the objectification of true being dissipates.

The World of *It*

It is possible to be taken in by the cadence of prose and depth of description without fully grasping what Buber is saying, when there is yet a deeper understanding at hand. Perhaps the best example of this in *I and Thou* is that of the alienated man encountered at the end of Part Two:

> ...if the man shudders at the alienation, and the *I* strikes terror in his heart, he looks up and sees a picture; which picture he sees does not matter, the empty *I* is stuffed full with the world or the stream of the world flows over it, and he is put at ease. But a moment comes, and it is near, when the shuddering man looks up and sees both pictures in a flash together. And a deeper shudder seizes him (72).

Is the alienated person "stuffed full with the world" like a straw-stuffed Scarecrow who scares away the birds but is recognized by the farmer as the image of a man, not the farmer himself? In other words, is the alienated person of whom it can be said the "stream of the world flows over" not a real person at all?

The person who would choose to escape the trappings of the world of the *It* and move toward authenticity, according to Buber, must be prepared for struggle:

> ...so is this man in the hours of reflection, shuddering, and aimlessly considering this and that...away in the unloved

knowledge of the depths of him, he really knows the direction of turning, leading through sacrifice (70).

Most often such innate knowledge is spurned for a more secure place in the order of reason and for a reliable picture of the world of objects. To escape the immediate abyss which threatens the bulwarks of an imagined reality which have fallen away must be rebuilt, even amidst the confession of a cowardliness to face the real *I* which is beckoned by the *Thou*. The single individual cries out:

I confess to you, it is empty, and whatever I do in myself, as a result of experiencing and using, does not fathom its emptiness (70).

And of unreality, the single individual asks:

Will you make it up between me and it, sot that it leaves off and I recover (70)?

It appears in a fitful dream to the surrendered reason of the alienated *I* and "ready with its service and its art, paints with its well-known speed one – no, two rows of pictures, on the right wall and on the left." One picture is of the universe and of a person being thrust through history frantically rebuilding one culture only to have it crushed by another. Beneath the picture is written the words, "One and all." The other picture is of the soul, the very heart of the individual, being thrust through history, entangled with its experiences, imaginings and sensations. Beneath the picture is written the words, "One and all."
If the alienated person becomes suddenly aware of the abyss, she needs only search her proper reason for either one of the picture images:

There he sees that the I is embedded in the world and that there is really no I at all – so the world can do nothing to the I, and [the] is put at ease; or he sees that the world is embedded in the I, and that there is really no world at all – so the world can do nothing do the I, and [she] is put at ease (72).

These are the two poles of the false self. At one extreme there is the unembodied self where the body is felt more as one object among other objects in the world than as the core of the individual's own being. Here the *I* becomes the *It* and can only relate to the *Thou* as an

It. The other extreme is the egoist for whom nothing is to be valued except one's own interests and pleasures. Here in this world of ontological insecurity is the mythological character Narcissus who pines away beside the pool; his love of and absorption with his reflection in the water drawing him toward his death and, in each passing moment, further away from the *Thou*.

Addressing the Eternal Thou

The *Thou* by its very nature is in no danger of becoming *It*. All avenues of true or false relation between person and person, person and *It*, and person and *Thou*, meet in the eternal *Thou* and all fulfillment and non-fulfilment finds consummation or desecration in the presence of direct relation with the *Thou*.

The most alienated of people, even the whole race of a people trapped in a culture of progress which relentlessly strives to identify them with the objects of its progess, can and often will in times of chaos attempt to address the *Thou*. Regardless of the illusion a person might hold of who the *Thou* is, of just how the *Thou* might choose to respond if a response were even to come, by the very grace which is its nature the *Thou* can be experienced:

> But when he, too, who abhors the name, and believes himself to be godless, gives his whole being to addressing the *Thou* of his life, as a *Thou* that cannot be limited by another, he addresses God (76).

Such grace concerns the "single one" of Buber addressed in the following chapter, but the single one must not concern itself with the arrival for such "grace concerns us in so far as we go out to it and persist in its presence; but it is not our object." It is the will which must concern the single one intent on true relation with the *Thou* and as one is confronted with the *Thou* one must "step into direct relation with it."

The activity of the person who enters with the whole being into true relation with the *Thou*, ironically appears as being at rest in the frenetic pace of the world, stable, prepared for a meeting in each moment of the day with nature, with others, with God. Experiences become secondary, as do the weight of ideas and values which place their demands on living.

If this is so, what is really necessary in this true union?:

...everything that has ever been devised and contrived in the time of the human spirit as precept, alleged preparation, practice, or meditation, has nothing to do with the primal, simple fact of the meeting. Whatever the advantages in knowledge or the wielding of power for which we have to thank this or that practice, none of this affects the meeting of which we are speaking; it all has its place in the world of *It* and does not lead one step, does not take *the* step, out of it (77).

True union is grasped by the complete acceptance of the *I* of the present moment. The *I* who is willing to give up the "false self-asserting instinct that makes a man flee to the possessing of things before the unreliable, perilous world of relation which has neither destiny nor duration and cannot be surveyed (78)."

5
Between Man and Man

In all ages it has undoubtedly been glimpsed that the reciprocal essential relationship between two beings signifies a primal opportunity of being, and one, in fact, that enters into the phenomenon that man exists. And it has also ever again been glimpsed that just through the fact that he enters into essential reciprocity, man becomes revealed as man; indeed, that only with this and through this does he attain to that valid participation in being that is reserved for him; thus, that the saying of Thou by the I stands in the origin of all individual human becoming (BM, 209).

Buber's Philosophical Anthropology

It can be daunting to encounter the raw material of Buber's philosophy in his early works *Daniel* and *I and Thou* without proper application to the various other fields of human experience he offers in his later works.

Between Man and Man and *The Knowledge of Man* are collections of essays from the mature philosophy of Buber which expound and enrich the principle of dialogue. Works from both periods of his life fill out and apply precision to the relation of the "essential spheres of life": our life with nature; our life with people; our life with spiritual beings.

The opening essay on "Dialogue" contrasts the concepts "dialogue" and "monologue" and through personal anecdotes Buber draws out a deeper understanding of his philosophy of dialogue. "The Question to the Single One" offers a fundamental critique of Kierkegaard's existentialism, especially regarding the Danish philosopher's attempt to create a relationship between the "Single One" and God which renders the relationship between person and person secondary.

In "Distance and Relation" Buber seeks to further the reader's understanding of dialogue and monologue as they concern the *I-Thou* relationship. If a person fails to enter into relation with the *Thou*, the distance between them "thickens and solidifies." Instead of room being

32

created for relation, the distance obstructs it. "Elements of the Interhuman" addresses the practical application of the theoretical component in "Distance and Relation." This essay also serves to complement the concept of the life of dialogue introduced early on. Here Buber is able to set the sphere of the "social" into the context where many individuals come together and are bound up into a collective culture of common experiences, without necessarily having to enter into deeper levels of intimacy which might create vulnerability.

The essay "Guilt and Guilt Feelings" forms the base of Buber's ethics and also serves as a critique of the therapeutic culture of our times. Buber attempts to explain the important differences existing between two types of guilt; "existential" and "real." The former is a socio-cultural phenomenon which fails to reach the individual at a level which is truly life-changing, while the latter represents that sort of guilt, most often repressed and unconscious, which is the source of true confession and a return to the authentic self.

Dialogue

Buber writes of a recurring dream he calls the "Dream of the Doublecry." The setting for the dream alternates between a primitive, vast cave, a mud building of some sort, and the edge of a gigantic forest. The beginning of the dream is often different, too, but the common theme running through the experience is the extraordinary events which occur to the dreamer:

> …with a small animal resembling a lion-cub (whose name I know in the dream but not when I awake) tearing the flesh from my arm and being forced only with an effort to loose its hold (1).

The duration of the terrible experience is lightning fast but then abruptly halts with Buber finding himself standing alone and crying out. The cry is the same in the dream each time, "inarticulate but in strict rhythm, rising and falling, swelling to a fullness which my throat could not endure were I awake, long and slow, quiet, quite slow and very long, a cry that is a song (1)." When the cry is over his heart stops beating.

In the distance another cry similar to his own can be heard:

> …it is not the same cry, certainly no "echo" of my cry but rather its true rejoinder…corresponding to mine, answering its tones – so much so, that mine, which at first had to my own ear no sound

of questioning at all, now appear as questions...which now all receive a response (2).

Each time the dream occurs the voices which the cries become are new and each time as the reply to his initial cry moves toward him, Buber experiences a sense of certitude that something life-changing has occurred; that "now it has happened":

> Nothing more. Just this, and in this way – *now it has happened.* If I should try to explain it, it means that that happening which gave rise to my cry has only now, with the rejoinder, really and undoubtedly happened (2).

At a point two years before writing down the details of his dream, however, something different takes place. In this particular dream, just at the point where his cry dies away and his heart stops beating and Buber anticipates the coming of the answering call, there is only silence. In the silence, caught off guard, a sudden realization of the meaning to the ongoing dream is manifest in such a degree Buber comes to understand it "with every pore of [his] body."

> As ever the rejoinder came in one of the earlier dreams this corresponded to and answered my cry. It exceeded the earlier rejoinder in an unknown perfection which is hard to define, for it resides in the fact that it was already there. When I had reached an end of receiving it, I felt again that certainty, pealing out more than ever, that *now it has happened* (3).

Silence as Communication

What has happened? In the recurring dream the echo of his cry is replaced by its absence and in the absence there comes a certainty experienced with every part of his being. What is this certainty? There is a conversation between two people that is beyond sound and gesture, Buber explains. To understand this silence where speech breaks down and a true understanding of what he means by dialogue, emerges we are to imagine two men sitting beside each other:

> They do not speak with one another, they do not look at one another, not once have they turned to one another. They are not in one another's confidence, the one knows nothing of the other's career, early that morning they got to know one another in the

course of their travels. In this moment neither is thinking of the other; we do not need to know what their thoughts are. The one is sitting on the common seat obviously after his usual manner, calm, hospitably disposed to everything that may come. His being seems to say it is too little to be ready, one must also be really *there*. The other, whose attitude does not betray him, is a man who holds himself in reserve, withholds himself. But if we know about him, that his withholding of himself is something other than an attitude, behind all attitude is entrenched the impenetrable inability to communicate himself. And now – let us imagine that this is one of the hours which succeed in bursting asunder the seven iron bands about our heart – imperceptibly the spell is lifted. But even now the man does not speak a word, does not stir a finger. Yet he does something. The lifting of the spell has happened to him – no matter from where – without his doing. But this is what he does now: he releases in himself a reserve over which only he himself has power. Unreservedly communication streams from him, and the silence bears it to his neighbor. Indeed it was intended for him, and he receives it unreservedly as he receives all genuine destiny that meets him. He will be able to tell no one, not even himself, what he has experienced. What does he now "know" of the other? No more knowing is needed. For where unreserved has ruled, even wordlessly, between men, the word of dialogue has happened sacramentally (4).

Human dialogue is tied up not only in the signs and signals which are the code of a language spoken but also in the very essence of the mystical coming together which occurs between individuals. Buber is convinced this embodiment of the dialogical principle is not easily explained to a reader in the context of ideas but, instead, from "the inmost recesses of the personal life (5)." If an understanding of Buber's concept of dialogue is unearthed in the context of experience, and he certainly leads us back to such personal encounters time and time again, one might be inclined to put aside the obvious objections to his argument, if only for a glimpse into his world.

There are three ways, according to Buber, in which a person perceives another right before their eyes. The *observer* watches and characterizes the facial expressions and gestures for clues into the thoughts and ideas of the one observed and is content in the role of voyeur. The *onlooker* is not the least bit concerned with the traits the subject possesses, but like the artist painting a portrait, the subject is not to be made a personal encounter. He must remain wholly other and objectified.

A third way of perception between persons is what Buber calls *becoming aware*. The onlooker and the observer share similar orientation in their positioning outside the subject viewing the other as an object "separated from themselves and their personal lives, who can in fact for this sole reason be 'properly' perceived (9)." Because of this orientation "what they experience in this way, whether it is, as with the observer, a sum of traits, or, as with the onlooker, an existence, neither demands action from them nor inflicts destiny on them. But rather the whole is given over to the aloof fields of aesthesis (9)," the nature and expression of an object.

Buber explains in another example of an encounter:

> It is a different matter when in a receptive hour of my personal life a man meets me about whom there is something, which I cannot grasp in any objective way at all, that "says something" to me. That does not mean, says to me what manner of man this is, what is going on in him, and the like. But it means, says something *to me*, addresses something to me, speaks something that enters my own life. It can be something about this man, for instance that he needs me. But it can also be something about myself. The man himself in his relation to me has nothing to do with what is said. He has no relation to me, he has indeed not noticed me at all. It is not he who says it to me, as that solitary man silently confessed his secret to his neighbor on the seat, but *it* says it (9).

Here Buber cannot describe, depict or denote this man who speaks in silence to him. In fact, to attempt to describe the man would be the end of the silent communication taking place between them. This "accepting" of all the possibilities of what may come from such an encounter while simultaneously trusting in the very moment that comes with the meeting is for Buber an understanding of what it means to *become aware* of what true dialogue is all about.

The Question to the Single One

Buber engages Kierkegaard's idea of the "single one" to contrast the idea of the Unique One put forth by Max Stirner, an English psychologist writing around the same time. Kierkegaard's own solitary life lived in early 19th century Copenhagen was itself marked by his unique self-created world of singleness which must be properly understood to grasp the concept of the "single one." Buber regards Kierkegaard's renunciation of fiancée Regina Olsen as the turning away from both women and the world in which women live. In this turning away the category of the single one is created; "the category through which, from the religious standpoint, time and history and the race must pass (40)."

In Kierkegaard's *The Point of View for my Work as an Author,* in the section of the work titled *Two Notes,* an explanation of the concept of the Single One emerges. Stirner's book *The Ego and his Own* concerned the idea of what Buber calls a "border concept" to the Single One – a concept which seeks to explain the meaning of the solitary life from a different perspective than Kierkegaard's. Buber strongly criticized this attempt and its author:

> Stirner, a pathetic nominalist and unmasker of ideas, wanted to dissolve the alleged remains of German idealism (as which he regarded Ludwig Feuerbach) by raising not the thinking subject nor man but the concrete present individual as "the exclusive I" to be the bearer of the world, that is, of "his" world. Here this Unique One "consuming himself" in "self-enjoyment" is the only one who has primary existence; only the man who comes to such a possession and consciousness of himself has primary existence – on account of the "unity and omnipotence of our I that is sufficient to itself, for it lets nothing be but itself (41)."

Here is the extreme pole of the solipsist explored earlier in *I and Thou,* the mythological Narcissus trapped in the world of ego, where the other and the *Thou* warrant no essential relationship. This person Stirner exhalts is for Buber "so empty of any genuine power to enter into relation only that it is better to describe as a relation only that in which not only *I* but also *Thou* can be said (41)."

Kierkegaard's concept of the Single One is similar to Stirner's Unique One only in the sense that they are both categories on the extreme of human relation. The Single One is the subject as concrete singularity much the same way in which the Unique one is the subject aware of its self in relation to every other person and thing surrounding it. The radical departure between the two, however, is that Kierkegaard's Single One is the self in search of self in the sense of *becoming aware* (to use Buber's terminology) and not in the sense of "knowing thyself" from a rational perspective, which is what Socratic wisdom was all about. Kierkegaard takes issue with the Greek concept of "knowing thyself."

Rational knowledge of one's self is merely religion masking itself as relationship with God, Kierkegaard believed:

> It is not a matter [becoming the Single One] of a condition of the soul, called religiosity. It is not a matter of existence in that strict sense in which – precisely by fulfilling the personal life – it steps in its essence over the boundary of the person. Then being, familiar being, becomes unfamiliar and no longer signifies my being but my participation in the Present Being (42).

Fundamentally, then, Kierkegaard's concept of the Single One corresponds to "all real human dealing with God." Kierkegaard's "alone" is not the alone of Stirner or Socarates, but the alone which Abraham experiences in Genesis 12:1, where he was told by his God to leave his country, his relatives, and his father's house to journey to a land unknown to him or in Genesis 22:2, where he is told to take his son Isaac to the land of Moriah, and offer him as a human sacrifice to this personal God as a sign of faith in their relationship.

Even mysticism cannot create this space Kierkegaard carves out for the Single One which Buber emphatically embraces as a foundation for his philosophy of dialogue. It is in mystical practice where the *I* can be absorbed and the Single One can cease to exist that such a philosophy set on preventing this union reveals that mysticism is merely tolerable of such subjectivity only long enough to watch it "radically melt away."

Is there really a way through such a narrow ridge? Is it possible to become this Single One? Kierkegaard writes:

> I myself do not assert of myself that I am that one. For I have indeed fought for it, but have not yet grasped it, and am in the continued fight continually reminded that it is beyond human strength to be 'the Single One' in the highest sense (49)."

Nonetheless, with the attitude which characterized Abraham, one of faith in believing a God of grace and mercy could somehow lead one on the path to becoming this Single One, to let oneself in humility and vulnerability succumb to being helped by God, one might realize this as a way toward its realization:

> All the enthusiasm of the philosophers for monologue, from Plato to Nietzsche, does not touch the simple experience of faith that speaking with God is something *toto genere* different from

38

"speaking with oneself"; whereas, remarkably, it is not something *toto genere* different from speaking with another human being (50).

"Then one became two," the idealist philosopher's expression of relationship or "one and one at one," the mystic's expression of relationship are two roads that can never be ontologically true. It is only in the relationship between two people that relate with their essential being where two people no longer are phenomenon to each other but become *Thou* to each other.

The Single One in Responsibility

The Single One in realizing the extraordinary circumstances of the world awakened must now choose to embrace that same world in order to touch "the realm of lightning and grace," existing beyond the mundane tasks of the day, yet, ironically, hidden within those tasks:

> The Single One who lives in his relation of faith must wish to have it fulfilled in the uncurtailed measure of the life he lives. He must face the hour which approaches him, the biographical and historical hour, just as it is, in its whole world content and apparently senseless contradiction, without weakening the impact of otherness in it. He must hear the message, stark and untransfigured, which is delivered to him out of this hour, presented by this situation as it arrives (65-6).

Reduction of this moment is not permitted, Buber argues. The Single One is not at liberty to choose a path out of the moment, the "whole cruel hour...at stake," which leads to a more secure or comfortable frame of reference. The whole of the moment claims the entire being of the Single One for itself. In this claim "however unharmoniously it strikes your ear" one must "give the answer from the depths, where a breath of what has been breathed in still hovers."

Buber writes:

> That man may not be lost there is need of the person's responsibility to truth in his historical situation. There is need of the Single One who stands over against all being which is present to him – and thus also over against the body politic – and guarantees all being which is present to him – and thus also the body politic (82).

True community and true commonwealth will be properly established only when the Single Ones become real and out of their actions through such a realization society-at-large is renewed.

Distance and Relation

Buber's most mature theoretical statement of philosophy of dialogue is put forth in his essay "Distance and Relation." He uses the terms "distance" and "relation" to further an understanding of the *I-It* and the *I-Thou* relationships.

The inner growth of the self does not occur in a vacuum. Ontological completion, as Buber refers to the process of inner growth, can happen only when another person is aware of his being understood by the other. A relationship with one's self will never bring about the desired growth toward unity with God and others. This can only be accomplished "pre-eminently in the mutuality of the making present – in the making present of another self and in the knowledge that one is made present in his own self by the other – together with the mutuality of acceptance, of affirmation and confirmation (71)."

Confirmation of our being by the other and a realization of our very presence in the being of the other are the essential desires of the human heart, Buber believes:

> The human person needs confirmation because man as man needs it. An animal does not need to be confirmed, for it is what it is unquestionably. It is different with man: Sent forth from the natural domain of species into the hazard of the solitary category, surrounded by the air of a chaos which came into being with him, secretly and bashfully he watches for a Yes which allows him to be and which can come to him only from one human person to another. It is from on man to another that the heavenly bread of self-being is passed (71).

This unqualified "Yes" which is the very principle of human life is realized in a sphere which Buber calls "making present." Wherever people come together to meet there is the potential for this concept to emerge but, unfortunately, it rarely does. For it to take place one is required to "imagine" the real, that is, in Buber's words, "I imagine to myself what another man is at this very moment wishing, feeling, perceiving, thinking, and not as a detached content but in his very reality, that is, as a living process in this man (70)." Everyone who comes together with a crowd of people or with one other person has this ability to "imagine" but not everyone chooses to exercise it.

For example, I attempt to imagine the pain a friend of mine is experiencing from the shocking loss of his teenage son to a rare disease. A year has passed since the loss, like a cyclone on a summer's day ripped through his life, when we come together. I avoid hollow sympathetic gestures and concentrate with all my being on the specific pain he manifests in his being, to become aware of it. Even without the description of his struggle, "this making present increases" in my soul "until it is a paradox" and he and I "are embraced by a common living situation." Buber writes:

> The pain which I inflict upon him surges up in myself, revealing the abyss of the contradictoriness of life between man and man. At such a moment something can come into being which cannot be built up in any other way (70).

On Genuine Conversation

The twofold principle of human life emerges in our relations to each other. This is the principle of "relation" over and against the principle of "distance." In the insect state, for example, in the working economy of the ant hill, there is no room for variation in the working order of the community, and there is no need for individual reward or acknowledgement as the individual is not recognized. In contrast, in human societies confirmation among each other is quite common even though there is a tendency in highly industrialized societies, as an example, to forego such confirmation and individual reward for the sake of production and progress of the object being produced. Buber writes:

> Man, as man, sets himself at a distance and makes him independent; he lets the life of men like himself go on round about him, and so he, and he alone, is able to enter into relation, in his own individual status, with those like himself. The basis of man's life with man is twofold, and it is one – the wish of every man to be confirmed as what he is, even as what he can become, by men; and the innate capacity in man to confirm his fellow men in this way (68).

Speech is the "great characteristic" of a person's relations and a witness to the closing of the gap created by distance between people. Genuine conversation signifies acceptance of the other among individuals, and when two people speak to each other with opposing viewpoints yet still endeavor to accept one another on the basis of being and not of opinion "the strictness and depth of human individuation, the elemental otherness of the other, is then not merely noted as the necessary starting point, but is affirmed form the one being to the other (69)."

When this occurs in speech:

> The desire to influence the other then does not mean the effort to change the other, to inject one's own "rightness" into him; but it means the effort to let that which is recognized as right, as just, as true (and for that very reason must also be established there, in the substance of the other) through one's influence take seed and grow in the form suited to individuation (69)."

Elements of the Interhuman

The practical application of the theoretical statement of Buber's mature philosophy in "Distance and Relation" is put forth in his essay "Elements of the Interhuman." The apparent dilemma between the silence of communication principle discussed in "Dialogue" and the purpose and power of genuine speech understood in "Distance and Relation" is addressed within the context of community.

In the course of genuine dialogue in community one may choose to speak or not, but in the process one may say many things through either mode. At the core of the communicative dialogue taking place, however, one must choose to be courageous enough to speak when speaking will bring about the *I-Thou* relation or choose silence if such a silence accomplishes the same purpose. There is never a foreknowing, when the opportunity for genuine dialog occurs, of whether silence or speech will serve best as "the course is of the spirit, and some discover what they have to say only when they catch the call of the spirit (87)."

It is assumed all the participants in the ideal situation above, where dialogue results in true relation, have an awareness of the presuppositions of genuine relating and are ready to honor these. When in the course of genuine dialogue a person or group of people attempts to withdraw or to dominate, a rash of serious problems are manifest and relationship breaks down.

Buber writes of such an event:

> I had a friend whom I account one of the most considerable men of our age. He was a master of conversation, and he loved it: his genuineness as a speaker was evident. But once it happened that

he was sitting with two friends and with the three wives, and a conversation arose in which by its nature the women were clearly not joining, although their presence in fact had a great influence. The conversation among the men soon developed into a duel between two of them (I was the third). The other "duelist," also a friend of mine, was of a noble nature; he too was a man of ture conversation, but given more to objective fairness than to the play of the intellect, and a stranger to any controversy. The friend whom I have called a master of conversation did not speak with his usual composure and strength, but he scintillated, he fought, he triumphed. The dialogue was destroyed (88).

The Social and the Interhuman

Being in society – being bound up in smaller communities which are in turn connected to larger communities which when combined create the so-called global community (a phenomenon of the 20th century) – certainly means that "each individual existence is enclosed and contained in a group existence (72)." It does not mean, however, that there necessarily exists between individual members of these communities any sort of individual relationship.

The idea of the "interhuman" crudely defined above, emerges out of Buber's delineation of the "sphere of the between," which he first defined as *das Zwischenmenschliche*, meaning the socio-psychological understanding of the life of people together in all its forms and actions, or in other words, "the social seen as a psychological process," ("What is Man? [1905]"). In "Elements of the Interhuman," Buber narrows the term interhuman to create a basis for his philosophy of dialogue and sets out to distinguish clearly between the unfortunate socialization of people unaccompanied by true relationship in the process of collectivization and the possibility of true socio-communal establishments where elements of personal relation vital to the growth and success of the society are not suppressed but encouraged.

The difference between the two societies became evident to Buber on one particular occasion:

I had joined the procession through a large town of a movement to which I did not belong. I did it out of sympathy for the tragic development which I sensed was at hand in the destiny of a friend who was one of the leaders of the movement. While the procession was forming, I conversed with him and with another, a goodhearted "wild man," who also had the mark of death upon

43

him. At that moment I still felt that the two men really were there, over against me, each of them a man near to me, near even in what was most remote from me; so different from me that my soul continually suffered from this difference, yet by virtue of this very difference confronting me with authentic being. Then the formations started off, and after a short time I was lifted out of all confrontation, drawn into the procession, falling in with its aimless step; and it was obviously the very same for the two with whom I had just exchanged human words. After a while we passed a café where I had been sitting the previous day with a musician whom I knew only slightly. The very moment we passed it the door opened, the musician stood on the threshold, saw me, apparently saw me alone, and waved to me. Straight-way it seemed to me as though I were taken out of the procession and of the presence of my marching friends, and set there, confronting the musician. I forgot that I was walking along with the same step; I felt that I was standing over there by the man who had called out to me, and without a word, with a smile of understanding, was answering him. When consciousness of the facts returned to me, the procession, with my companions and myself at its head, had left the café behind (73-4).

This "drawing out" of community and being drawn into the personality of the individual standing before us, beyond the impersonal realm of the interhuman and into the immediate state of relation with another, is for Buber the true ground of the space that exists between person and person, between the objectivity of the *It* and the presence of the *Thou*.

Guilt and Guilt Feelings

"...I repeat, the psychotherapist in his medical intercourse with his patients has nothing to do, not even when he ventures in a particular case to set for himself the goal of an existential healing. The utmost that can be expected of him, as I have said, is only this: that, reaching out beyond his familiar methods, he conduct the patient, whose existential guilt he has recognized, to where an existential help of the self can begin. But to do this, he must know about the reality I have tried to point out...(148)"

In his essay "Guilt and Guilt Feelings" Buber indicts the psychotherapeutic culture of our time while establishing a strong basis for his ethical philosophy. "The Genesis of Guilt" was the theme at the

London International Conference for Medical Psychotherapy in 1948 and the springboard into the theme of this work. Buber notes there was confusion throughout the session over whether or not the actual subject up for discussion was the *genesis of guilt* or the *genesis of guilt "feelings."* Although the question remained unclarified throughout the conference it worked itself out in such a way that the theologians involved were left to speak of guilt itself while the psychologists concentrated on the concept of guilt feelings. Buber writes:

> This distribution of themes, through which the factual occurrences of guilt in the lives of "patients," of suffering men, hardly enters into view, is characteristic of most of what one calls the psychotherapeutic discipline. Only in the most recent period have some begun to complain that both in the theory and in the practice of this science the psychic "projection" of guilt is afforded room, the real events of guilt are not (121).

Buber believes the "real events of guilt" are the places in the psyche of the patient no psychotherapist need ever be concerned with if the choice is made to remain unattached from the patient's deepest fears and hopes for renewal. Should the therapist choose to explore these events, however, there must be a willingness to accept a relationship with the patient moving beyond the superficial limits imposed by the profession and to accept such a relationship as a "reciprocal reality" that transcends both the task and the method applied to bring about growth. The therapist must "cast his glance again and again to where existing person relates to existing person – this person, the "patient," to another living being who is not "given" to the doctor and who may be completely unknown to him (122)."

Freud and Jung

Buber explores the work of two notable representatives of the school of psychoanalysis, Freud and Jung, in order to come to an understanding of the motivations behind its historical embrace of this existential guilt.

The boundaries set, or the removal of boundaries between the patient and the therapist, are not enough to explain the ontological character of the existential guilt the psychotherapeutic community has substituted for the real guilt Buber embraces.

Freud recognized the necessity of defining guilt in terms of society's struggle with the repressive structures of religion imposing an absolute moral order upon its subjects. Guilt became a result of a fear of punishment from this absolute:

> The first renunciation of instinctual gratification is enforced by external powers, and it is this that creates morality which expresses itself in conscience and exacts a further renunciation of instinct (*Collected Papers*, 255-268).

Jung's teaching regarding guilt is diametrically opposed to that of Freud. He embraces the religious aspects of guilt as grist for the mill of psychoanalytic theory itself but admits such aspects are to be considered "projections" of the psyche, creations born out of illusion and taboo.

Freud allows the superego to be the heart of the psyche where the structures of society and family impose upon the individual the moral absolute, while Jungian guilt is entangled in the self which is the individual as subject creating a subjective sense of guilt easily grasped through subjective experience.

Jung cannot, in his anthropology, recognize a relationship between two individuals which moves beyond the psychic dimension. According to Buber, Jung receives the label of panpsychism, the idea that a mental element is present in everything and between everyone that exists. Panpsychism has also been used as a synonym for immaterialism which brings one back around to Freud's material theory of guilt, where society and taboo, through socio-cultural interaction with the individual, infuse a sense of dread into the controlling superego.

According to Buber, existential guilt – guilt an individual is willing to take responsibility for – is not to be understood under the scientific categories of Freud's "repression" or Jung's collective consciousness. A doctor who is honest with himself and his patient, with his patient and the patient's place in the world will have to face the fact that a reality exists beyond any methodology he is learned in, "a reality beyond, inaccessible to any of the psychological categories (128)."

If the therapist comes to term with this reality, Buber writes, then she has done a great service to her profession and to her patient, yet, simultaneously, "all that she is obliged to do becomes more difficult, much more difficult – and all becomes more real, radically real (128)."

A "Genius of Friendship"

A case study of one of Buber's acquaintances is revealing. In its entirety, the fate of Melanie before and after her encounter with psychoanalysis delivers Buber's criticism of the industry with damning precision:

> The life course I have in mind is that of a woman – let us call her Melanie – of more intellectual than truly spiritual gifts, with a scientific education, but without the capacity for independent mastery of her knowledge. Melanie possessed a remarkable talent for good comradeship which expressed itself, at least from her side, in more or less erotically tinged friendships that left unsatisfied her impetuous rather than passionate need for love. She made the acquaintance of a man who was on the point of marriage with another, strikingly ugly, but remarkable woman. Melanie succeeded without difficulty in breaking up the engagement and marrying the man. Her rival tried to kill herself. Melanie soon afterwards accused her, certainly unjustly, of feigning her attempt at suicide. After a few years Melanie herself was supplanted by another woman. Soon Melanie fell ill with a neurosis linked with disturbances of the vision. To friends who took her in at the time, she confessed her guilt without glossing over the fact that it had arisen not out of a passion, but out of a fixed will.
>
> Later she gave herself into the care of well-known psychoanalyst. This man was able to liberate her in a short while from her feelings of disappointment and guilt and to bring her to the conviction that she was a "genius of friendship" and would find in this sphere the compensation that was due her. The conversion succeeded, and Melanie devoted herself to a rich sociality which she experienced as a world of friendship. In contrast to this, she associated in general with the men with whom she had to deal in her professional "welfare work" not as persons needing her understanding and even her consolation, but as objects to be seen through and directed by her. The guilt feelings were no longer in evidence; the apparatus that had been installed in place of the paining and admonishing heart functioned in model fashion (128-9).

Melanie's guilt feelings were silenced, supposedly, and a new world of promise opens up for her. Or does it? Buber argues that the authenticity

47

which originally accompanied Melanie's guilt feelings, once silenced, no longer allowed for the "possibility of reconciliation through a newly won genuine relationship to her environment in which her best qualities could at the same time unfold (129)."

The price Melanie pays for the silence of guilt, what Buber calls the "annihilation of the sting," is the loss of a chance to become aware of who she really is meant to be.

A Glimpse of the Way

The therapist is not responsible for showing the patient her way into the world and out of the existential guilt weighing down the spirit. She can only guide the patient to a place where taking responsibility for one's own guilt and for one's actions and the consequences thereof becomes a real beginning to a new way to experience existence.

There are three spheres which it is possible for existential guilt to find a path toward reconciliation and individual relationships take on true and proper meaning in the moment of the real. Of these three spheres there is only one that is the proper concern of the therapist.

The first sphere regards society's rule of law, in which guilt is discovered through the investigative branch or through the individual's coming forward under moral duress to make a confession. A judgment follows confession and the guilt is recorded as a future reminder to the individual and society of the breach of contract. In this sphere the psychotherapist has no jurisdiction.

The third and highest sphere is that of faith. Through the realization of sin, the act of repentance and, in certain faiths, the act of penance, a person submits to the guilt experienced before God. In this sphere the therapist "cannot interfere...even if he posseses great spiritual gifts – without falling into a dangerous dilettantism (134)."

The middle sphere allows the therapist to approach its boundary, but not beyond. This is the sphere of *conscience*. Buber writes:

> Conscience means to us the capacity and tendency of man radically to distinguish between those of his past and future actions which should be approved and those which should be disapproved (134).

Here the therapist can assist, whether or not neurotic behavior is involved, in the awakening of a patient in the throes of anguish precipitated by the work of conscience. The assistance should bring the patient to a place of threefold action Buber outlines:

...first, to illuminate the darkness that still weaves itself about the guilt despite all previous action of the conscience – not to illuminate it with spotlights but with a broad and enduring wave of light; second, to perservere, no matter how high he may have ascended in his present life above that station of guilt – to persevere in that newly won humble knowledge of the identity of the present person with the person of that time; and third, in his place and according to his capacity, in the given historical and biographical situations, to restore the order-of-being injured by him through the relation of an active devotion to the world – for the wounds of the order-of-being can be healed in infinitely many other places than those at which they were inflicted (136).

In order to restore this order-of-being, however, the person working through real guilt and the consequences of negative actions must strive to protect each new chapter of unity which comes through confession and surrender and must fight with courage to, first and foremost, attain the real self. Only in the acquisition of this self can good follow and not the other way around.

Stavrogin

When the guilty person suddenly comes to terms with the guilt within, there is a realization of trespass on both the societal level as the confession of guilt before the court of law and on the spiritual level as the confession of guilt before the law of God.

As the modern person's self-enlightenment grows through the promise of the power of reason to create a world where guilt is a by-product of religious imagination, the idea that there is an absolute to answer to, much less an absolute who enforces an absolute rule of law, becomes increasingly more difficult to ascend to:

...it has become more difficult for the man of our age than any earlier one to venture self-illumination with awake and unafraid spirit, although he imagines that he knows more about himself than did the man of any earlier time (138).

Buber turns to the characters Nikolai Stavrogin in Dostoevski's novel *The Possessed,* (1870), and Joseph K. in Franz Kafka's narrative *The Trail,* (1915), as perfect examples of this modern day dilemma.

In the original novel Stavrogin, who has become absolutely corrupted by his abuse of power, visits a priest with the hopes of having his written confession published – a confession which among other appalling deeds includes the rape of a little girl. Although the confession itself is accurate, Stavrogin knows the act of delivering it lacks true contrition. What he is looking for is a magical way out of his guilt. "Would it be impossible to do it suddenly?" he asks. "Impossible?" the priest replies. "From the work of an angel it would become the work of a devil." "Ah," Stavrogin exclaims, "that I already knew myself."

Confession and crime are committed by Stavrogin in much the same spirit: "as an attempt to snatch the genuine existence which he does not possess, but which – nihilist in practice but (in anticipation) existentialist in views – he has recognized as the true good. He is full of "ideas," full of "spirit," but he does not exist (139)."

Joseph K.

The question asked in Kafka's *Trail* (1915) closely associated with the "uncanny negative certainty" that "human values are beginning to shatter," according to Buber, is whether or not the "world-meaning and world-order still have any connection at all with this nonsense and this disorder of the human world (140)?"

Joseph K. shoulders a burden of guilt he is not sure he has earned but, nonetheless, continues to go about his daily life lacking any direction except for the only thing which seems to offer him motivation: the desire to be free of the burden of the law pressing down upon him. Eventually he is on the verge of making a false confession to the court aware that he is guiltless simply because he takes the advice of a woman who seems to be wise in the ways of the process of justice. At this point, however, Joseph K encounters a painter who too seems to know the ways of the court. He advises him that the burden of proof is not on his guiltless disposition and that if he is in fact innocent than innocence will represent him well.

Buber highlights Joseph K.'s encounter with a priest in the chapter "In the Cathedral," which parallels with striking accuracy the account of its kind already discussed with Stavrogin in *The Possessed*. Buber writes:

> In both a priest is the antagonist, in both it is a matter of a confession of guilt; however, in Dostoevski it is furnished undemanded while in Kafka it is demanded. For it is this demand that the chaplain wishes to convey by the information that the case is going badly, since the court holds the guilt to be proved (142).

"But I am not guilty," answers K., "it's a misunderstanding. And, if it comes to that, how can any man be called guilty? We are all simply men here, one as much as the other (142)."

The priest replies, "This is true. But that's how all guilty men talk."

Joseph K. refuses to believe there is such a thing as guilt and in his confession "we are all simply men here" is his way of refusing to allow the inner light of true confession to shine its rays of release upon the meaninglessness of his life.

Self-Illumination

The destinies of Joseph K and Stavrogin are inextricably intertwined with the false relationships they both entertain in order to engage, or to dis-engage their own guiltiness. Buber writes:

> It is the crucial hour of man of which we speak. For, to use Pascal's language, the greatness of man is bound up with his misery. Man is the being who is capable of becoming guilty and is capable of illuminating his guilt (146).

There exists, however, a fundamental difference between the types of guilt Joseph K and Stavrogin struggle with and the sort of guilt the patient experiences in the therapeutic relationship. The fictitious characters are both fully aware of the possibility of guilt and its attribution of such guilt to them on a conscious level, but refuse or choose to relegate the concept of guilt itself to a realm of mythology and idealism which cannot possibly impinge upon the supposed reality they create within themselves. Theirs is a place of relative existence which simply mirrors the chaos of the shattered world around them. In dangerous times people are allowed to take their chances with reality, since reality itself seems to be in question.

For the patient in the psychoanalytic environment today there is the so-called repressed guilt which must be summoned up from its unconscious cellar and into the light of the conscious existence of the individual who is surprised of its arrival upon the landscape of memory:

> It is not for me to speak in general terms of the inner reality of him who refuses to believe in a transcendent being with whom he can communicate. I have only this to report: that I have met many

men in the course of my life who have told me how, acting from the high conscience as men who had become guilty, they experienced themselves as seized by a higher power (148).

These men, Buber writes, "grew into an existential state to which the name of rebirth is due (148)."

6

Hasidism and the Modern Man

In order to come to know the radical difference between the intensely intimate God of Abraham, Isaac and Jacob and the rational God of the philosophers, the 26-year-old Buber withdraws from his active life of writing and lecturing and an intensive study of Jewish sources to immerse himself in the teachings of Hasidism from 1904 to 1909, the next five years of his life.

Hasidism comes from the Hebrew word *Hasid* which is translated as "a pious one." It was founded in the villages of Poland in the middle of the eighteenth century by Israel ben Eliezer (1700-1760) – also known as the Baal Shem Tov, or "Master of the Good Name" (the name of God). Promoted throughout Eastern Europe among traditional Jews living according to the simple philosophy of their founding fathers, over one-hundred-and-fifty years of history stood between its staunch adherents and their absolute allegiance to the God of Israel and modern day society.

As a boy, Buber grew up around communities practicing the Hasidic way of life, and it was in his boyhood days that an indelible impression of the community *esprit de corps* practiced by the Hasidic people would influence him in such a way as to effect his comprehensive view of life.

Buber became especially fascinated with the Hasidic history of the 18th century, specifically the Eastern European school of Judaic Mysticism founded by Israel ben Eliezer. In the seventy-five years between 1750 and 1825 there had been a phenomenal growth in Hasidic communities across Europe. The vast wealth of literature and documentation of this period was for Buber a treasure chest of historical data which needed to be synthesized into a readily accessible body of work capable of inspiring Jewish people around the world. For

Buber the Hasidic way of life, if properly disseminated among the Jewish people, could be a much needed source of renewal:

> Since I began my work on Hasidic literature, I have done this work for the sake of the teaching and the way. But at that time I believed that one might relate to them merely as an observer. Since then I have realized that the teaching is there so that one might learn it and the way that one might walk in it. The deeper I realized this, so much more the work, against which my life measured and ventured itself, became for me question, suffering, and also even consolation (HM, 25).

As is often the case with mystic religious interests, the tendency to examine the profound and lofty ambitions of the ecstatic experience can work against the present vitality of the practical and timely. This tendency could not be farther from Buber's concerns relative to the Hasidic perspective, which he understands in the inwardness of the here and now, a realized Judaism encountering the presence and essence of the divine demand in the everyday.

The Divine Spark

The holy sparks that fell when God built and destroyed worlds, man shall raise and purify upward from stone to plant, from plant to animal, from animal to speaking being, purify the holy sparks that are imprisoned in the world of shells. That is the basic meaning of each one in Israel (187).

God makes his dwelling in the midst of a sinful and suffering creation, among the many deceptions and desperations of men. The presence of God exists in exile. The essence of God remains removed from the secular sphere, withdrawn and ineffable. However, the divine presence lingers in created world, scattered and stray, as the *Shekina*, the divine spark which stoops in the soul as if prematurely entombed.

The shards of *Shekina* inhabit all that takes shape and substance in the created world, from oxcarts to kings, desiring only that reunification with the divine source which results in existential singularity. To participate in this reunification, to undertake ownership and administration of the form or object for the sake of the *Shekina* urge constitutes the very heart of human holiness. To this end, man does not approach the divine demand through any agency outside of the visceral continuity of human history. Quite to the contrary, men were created to be human, to be perfected in the unconditioned characteristic of humanity. Therefore, to exercise appropriate dominion for the sake of the *Shekina*, to administrate one's environment as an enterprise participating in the redemption of divine indwelling in even the most mundane of implements and interests, is to engage the grace of the God who comes, to be purified at the root of the human essence.

For the Hasidim, there is no irreconcilable argument between that which is sacred and that which is profane. The blessing of God is appropriately invoked at the introduction of even the most menial resource or in the reality of the least significant moment. The profane is merely a "preliminary stage" of the sacred, that which is not yet hallowed. Come the end of days, the messianic kingdom, and all will be holy, all will exist in essential unity. Such is the mysterious grace of God that it is given to men to participate in the progression to this culminating singularity, to liberate and escort the imprisoned *Shekina* to their source in the *Elohim*, the encompassing presence of God.

The *Shekina* ever awaits freedom to the end of redemption. The world awaits the pious one, the "conveyor of the divine spark," the Hasidim, through whom worlds are sewn into focus and the redemptive design moves forth.

Four Principles of Hasidism

The mystery of grace cannot be interpreted. Between seeking and finding lies the tension of the human life, indeed the thousandfold return of the anxious, wandering soul. And yet the flight of the moment is slower than the fulfillment. For God wishes to be sought, and how could he not wish to be found (85).

Buber isolates four interactive principles forming a foundation of the Hasidic way of life, of religious reality and experience: *Hitlahavut* (the inflaming), *avoda* (service), *kavana* (intention) and *shiflut* (humility). Each of these principles participate in the hallowing of the Hasidic heart, where hallowing denotes a deeper experience of essential humanity. To draw near to God, to experience the "stilling" of suffering is not to transcend one's humanity but to realize and clarify that which is existentially and actually human to the root. The Hasidic heart, then, does not transcend the natural. It does, however, open itself to the habitation of the condescending divine. This *teshuvah* (turning) occurs in accordance with the Hasidic saying: *God dwells where one lets Him in.*

Hitlahavut, religious ecstasy, is an encounter and "envelopment by God beyond space and time", the mystical experience of the unadulterated divine (84). *Hitlahavut* is the progressive elevation of the individual identity into the encounter and embrace of the infinite, the way without end:

> When man moves from strength to strength and ever upward and upward until he comes to the root of all teaching and all command, to the I of God, the simple unity and boundlessness-when he stands there, then all the wings of command and law sink down and are as if destroyed. For the evil impulse is destroyed since he stands above it (77).

The Hasidic experience of *Hitlahavut* presupposes human movement through progressive spheres of mystical experience, each encompassing the last. The angelic being finds its rest in God, but man moves forward in him. In this much, man is greater than the angels.

Hitlahavut presupposes this velocity of the Hasidic identity. In many instances, the heart of the Hasidic experience of *Hitlahavut* hinges upon the essential element of individual isolation, wandering and dispossession. Buber describes those "unsettled and fugitive" individuals who move into exile in order to express an essential sympathy with the *Shekina*, also thought of as the endlessly wandering glory of God in exile.

Hitlahavut, in and of itself, is not an ascetic interest but an overcoming of the lower sphere, not a beyond but an above, an overwhelming unity allowing the individual a mastery of life in meaning and in practice. The Old Testament describes a sword of fire guarding the gates to paradise. *Hitlahavut* scatters that sword to sparks, revealing in all things of the world the strength and pride of the Creator, against which no alternative can stand. *Hitlahavut* is silent and substantive, a dwelling in the heart of God, revealing its most intimate rapture in the suspension of its own sensation, streaming from search to discovery, pursuit to peace.

Beneath the *Hitlahavut* is the *avoda*, the service of God within the continuum of space and time, in creative history. Where *Hitlahavut* is fulfillment *avoda* is longing. *Avoda* is the organizing principle which conducts chaos to certainty, multiplicity to unity. Buber approaches *avoda* in terms of the realized creative impulse, originating in God and mirrored in men:

> God governs men as He governed chaos at the time of the infancy of the world. "And as when the world began to unfold and He saw that if it flowed further asunder it would no longer be able to return to its roots, then he spoke, 'Enough!'- so is it that when the soul of man in its suffering rushes headlong, without direction, and evil becomes so mighty in it that it soon could no longer return home, then His compassion awakes, and he says, 'Enough!'" (85-6).

In a similar fashion, man too collects himself into an individualized unity against a myriad of inner multiplicities, divisions and contradictions. It is in this existential "Enough!" that man participates in the oneness of God. This, then, is a return to the unconditioned root of self. As stated before, to encounter the divine is to actualize that which is most deeply human in men.

Man, according to Buber, does not only participate existentially in the oneness of God, but also participates experientially in the restoration of the divine oneness which has fallen into duality through the creative consequence. The essence of God (*Elohim*) remains withdrawn from the created world, while the presence of God (*Shekina*) lingers in the midst of men as if in exile, disposed, scattered and transient. It is a grace to men that they have been given into the service of a relatively redemptive stratagem, escorting the shards of *Shekina* to their essential source.

The presence of God yearns towards this reunification, this oneness, and so the *avoda* constitutes those acts of service which men undertake for the sake of the *Shekina* urge. As Buber notes "only the prayer that takes place for the sake of the *Shekina* truly lives (88)." Prayer is only efficacious inasmuch as it moves beyond the suffering of self and addresses the desired reunification of the higher root, the essence and presence of God. This is not intended to suggest the necessity of intellectual exercise. God most adores the prayers of simple men, the "unbroken promptings" of the unified human heart. Every act of service which proceeds from the undivided soul is "sufficient and complete (94)."

Where *Hitlahavut* is an intimate and individualized experience, *avoda* encompasses the communal dynamic. An individual prayer, for example, may be inhibited by its underlying intention or by the earlier misdeeds of the praying man. In such a case, the praying man must either ascend into the ecstatic sphere so that his prayers may be purified by grace or, as an alternative, have his prayers carried upward along with those of another individual who is in *Hitlahavut*, in the ecstatic embrace of the divine.

The souls of men "bind themselves to one another for greater unity and might (91)." The image of community, then, is that of a vertical chain of which each man is a necessary link, one higher than the next, all straining upward to the ecstatic envelopment of the divine and all-entangling the scattered *Shekina*, drawing it down, collecting it into a culminating unity. There is a sort of service to God beyond the ability of the individual.

Kavana is the mysterious intention or goal of the human soul. To guide the soul or the imprisoned sparks of the soul to their source in the divine essence is to participate in the perfection of their intended aim. There is only one true goal, that of redemption:

> This is the way of redemption, that all souls and all sparks of souls which have sprung up from the primeval soul and have sunk and become scattered in all creatures at the time of the original darkening of the world or through the guilt of the ages should conclude their wandering and return home purified (101).

The *Shekina* remains imprisoned in the forms of the created world, in all that exists. It is incumbent upon men to participate in their liberation in accordance with the redemptive design, to set them in motion towards *Elohim*, the essential source. Each individual is endowed with a sphere of redemptive influence, a natural environment containing artifacts in which are suspended the scattered sparks of *Shekina*, those animals and artifacts which constitute personal possession.

To oversee and utilize this circle of resource in holiness is to participate in the liberation of that imprisoned presence of the divine within them, a redemptive dedication. As the individual engages God within the circumstance of life, sparks of the scattered *Shekina* present themselves to him, desiring to be raised and redeemed by him. These sparks belong to the man of holiness and, in becoming their conduit and escort, the man receives his inner enjoyment of them. Buber refers to this as the *kavana* of receiving; "that one redeem the sparks in the surrounding things and the sparks that draw near out of the invisible (106)."

There is also the *kavana* of giving, that which has its goal in the submission of self to the infinite and progresses of a course to the ecstatic envelopment, into *Hitlahavut*. This *kavana* finds its actuality in the creative power of the word, of the orchestrated voice. For the Hasidim, the power of speech is both mysterious and astonishing. The voice is a chaos that the speaker organizes to a morphology of meaning. In this the spoken word is a direct reflection of that creative capability which first formulates in the divine:

> "One should speak words as if the heavens were opened in them.
> And as if it were not so that you take the word in your mouth, but
> rather as if you entered the word." He who knows the secret
> melody that bears the inner to the outer, who knows the holy song
> that merges the lonely, shy letters into the singing of the spheres,
> he is full of the power of God, "and it is as if he created heaven
> and earth and all the worlds anew (107)."

As established, there is only one true goal, that of redemption. Stated in another form, there is only one true meaning, one verified intention, that of the essential return. Speech, then, is a form of creation and, just as the essence of God inhabits the creation drawn from void, so does the soul of the speaker inhabit the spoken word. In this creative capacity, the holy words of man unite themselves to God in "genuine unity, since a man has set his soul in them, and worlds unite themselves and ascend, and the great rapture is born (107)." The receptive *kavana*, that which redeems, and the contributive *kavana*, that which creates, constitute the essential will of the Hasidic identity.

Shiflut, or humility, encompasses the Hasidic interest in appropriate self-perception relative to human identity in relationship to other men and to God. Each living soul is unique, incomparable. The pursuit of essential unity, the redemptive desire, perfects that inherent individuality, removing the identity from the dividing influence of otherness.

The individual seeks God as an individual, in "lonely fervor," laying hold of his own, unique character and acting out of his own sublimely specialized nature. However, even the perfection of the individual functions to the end of the communal interest, as is the case with the ascent to *Hitlahavut*, where one man may take upon his own character the burden of another's struggling attempts towards the ecstatic envelopment of God. The individual is unique, but not self-sufficient:

> The individual sees God and embraces Him. The individual redeems the fallen worlds. And yet the individual is not a whole, but a part. And the purer and more perfect he is, so much more intimately does he know that he is a part and so much the more actively there stirs in him the community of existence. That is the mystery of humility (112).

To draw near to God is to draw near to one's essential humanity, to perfect one's unique identity towards the aim of essential unity. However, a narrowing proximity to one's own essential humanity must necessarily promote existential identification with the human community, those who share and participate in that humanity. This humility is not tinged with self-deprecation, does not lower itself beneath the reality of actual status. This humility does not contrast individual identity against an alternative, against the other.

To rightly recognize the specialized characteristics of the Other is to see without condemnation the soul of the individual in the splendor of its particular existence. At this level of existential identification, service to another is not a task, but a matter of course. Thus, Hasidic humility is not a self-imposed standard of social conscience, not a restraint, but an outpouring of the indivisible spirit as natural as "the glance of a child and as simple as a child's speech (115)."

The unified individual remains untouched by all in his entirely unique individual identity and yet embraced by all in the deepening certainty of his essential humanity, both separate and inseparable, unblemished by shallow sympathies. In each human soul rests a spark of the original soul, of the presence of God in the midst of humanity. In each spark lies the yearning for the whole.

The Aim of the Human Heart

But also in man, in every man, is a force divine. And in man far more than in all other beings it can pervert itself, can be misused by himself. This happens if he, instead of directing it towards its origin, allows it to run directionless and seize at everything that offers itself to it: instead of hallowing passion, he makes it evil. But here, too, a way to redemption is open: he who with the entire force of his being "turns" to God, at this his point of the universe lifts the divine immanence out of its debasement, which he has caused (127).

In the Hasidic perspective the ideal relationship with God is not achieved through ascetic enterprise or the renunciation of natural being but in its truest affirmation. The passion, when properly directed to its point of origin in the divine, is made holy, affirming the individual desire for the sake of God in whom rests the primeval desire, the first among inclinations. In God remains the only veritable aim and end of the human heart.

To some extent, however, that aim and end is particular to the individual. As Buber notes, "each person born into this world represents something new. Something that never existed before (139)." To this end, it is incumbent upon the individual to walk in that particular way specialized to his or her own inner existence:

God does not say: "This way leads to me and that does not," but he says: "Whatever you do may be a way to me, provided you do it in such a manner that it leads to me." But what it is that can and shall be done by just this person and no other can be revealed to him only in himself (141).

To this end, it is inappropriate to assume the popular posture, to understand one's own potentiality and purpose in the light of the accomplishments of another. Any natural act, undertaken for the sake of God, if performed in an appropriate way, guides the individual into the actualization of his or her own inwardness and uniqueness. From out of this actualization flows the binding humanity at the core of true community. Likewise, preoccupation with self is an inhibiting factor in the actualization of self. One must not pursue the redemptive design for the sake of personal interest or the perfection of individual identity, but for the sake of the design, itself, for the sake of the holy spark.

Hasidism understands the created form as vessel. Each form contains the imprisoned essence of the *Shekina*, the shards of that divine presence which rained down within the context of the creative act. In a sense, this perspective is privative in foundation. There exists only one legitimate yearning, one independent principle, that of redemption, the return to the singular source in God. Evil rests in the resistance of this unifying inclination. To correct the corrupted course of the straying *Shekina* is to redeem some portion of the world.

Hasidism, as Buber engages and recreates it, must be approached within the context of the immediate, the vitality of the here and now. It is a religious reality rooted in the practical pursuit of personal holiness and the hallowing of the everyday. It is through this hallowing that the individual achieves communal utility, offering up a unique and immediate individuality as commodity to the continuity of blood.

Buber's encounter with Hasidism, which emphasized joyful worship of God in the here and now of this world and this life, transformed him from a European intellectual, groping for Jewish roots, into a thinker whose cast of mind and deepest loyalties were indelibly Jewish. His characterization of the prophets of Israel as "national-universalists" applies equally to him. His passionate concern for humanity is rooted in the particularity of his loyalty to his people and their faith, but, even as important to him, his loyalty to the hallowing of everyday life in all individuals he might come into contact with.

Throughout Buber's long life (February 8, 1978 to June 13, 1965) in both his early existential philosophy and the mature religious existential work, the theme of carefully navigating the narrow rocky ridge cutting through the center of the struggles of communal utility and individual autonomy is apparent. The connection between his actual life and the subsequent development of his philosophy is evident even in the formative years, to which we now turn our attention.

7
Judaism

Buber approaches Judaism as a phenomenon of religious reality. One may understand Judaism in its contemporary or historical context as culture or cult, but any acceptable definition of Judaism must be rooted in the religious reality which is core to the experience (becoming) and expression (being) of the Jewish identity. This is not to suggest that the divine is actualized in human experience. This religious reality does not occur within the inner life of man.

The divine is necessarily self-actualizing in essence and expression and may be encountered by man, but never possessed by him. Rather, Buber's religious reality occurs, as does all dialogue, in the space between man and the divine, in the relationship, itself. From this space grows Buber's desire to differentiate between Torah as law and Torah as revelation, the Jew as exile (*galut*) and elemental (*Urjuden*), Jewish religion and Jewish religiosity. In all matters, Buber aspires to that Judaism which is a unity (*Einheit*) of conceptualization and yearning, a Judaism of genuine and active unitary tendency in which the adoration between Jew and God informs and enlivens doctrine.

Theophany, or the visible manifestation of the divine in history, accounts for the existence of the Judaic religious reality. At the core of theophany rests the immutable and revelatory essence of the divine, committed into the possession of men as image and idea subsequently and structurally determined at many turns by external shifts in cultural and historical perspective.

Buber is keenly aware of a contemporary tendency to view the divine as a consequence of human creativity occupied in recognizable cultural enterprise. That is, religion might be understood as a semi-artistic satisfaction of various issues of moral, spiritual and aesthetic integrity and understanding rooted in the insecurities of individuals in human community, a necessary fiction. To this end, it would be appropriate to proceed "as if" god existed. In such a case, Buber notes, it would also be appropriate for god to proceed "as if" the feigner did not.

Thus, the primary conflict relative to the religious reality becomes that between the being of God as revealed and the becoming of God as interpreted by the human recipients of revelation and their heirs. The recollection of God's presence informs the subsequent history of a religious reality, in which both man and God participate. Evolving cultural and historical influences do not operate at the core of this religious reality. Rather, they are an externally imposed and progressive limitation upon the revitalizing substance of revelation.

At the core of the Judaic religious reality is the revelation of the being of the divine. Men may look "over there" for a sign or semblance of divinity, only to discover the god who speaks "from here", from the very heart of the unconditioned Jew. All men may be to some extent aware of an encounter with the divine. The Jew, however, must always be aware of this encounter, driven by theophany in their inmost certainty, relating to god in the "immediacy of the I and Thou – as a Jew." From his or her most unafraid and honest I, the Jew gives volition to the destiny of god on earth.

The sun projects light which is subsequently quantified by the human eye as bright, dim or some other variant of perception. Still, light in essence occurs between star and sight regardless of human perspective. In much the same way, the essence of revelation, the source of Judaism, is discovered in the space between divine emanation and human interpretation.

Judaism and the Jewish Identity

...It is time's great heritage that we bring with us into the world. We Jews need to know that our being and our character have been formed not solely by the nature of our fathers but also by their fate, and by their pain, their misery and humiliation. We must feel this as well as know it, just as we must feel and know that within us dwells the element of the prophets, the psalmist, and the kings of Judah (J, 17).

The child moves toward an unconditioned understanding that the *I* is contained within the world. The adult moves forward to an unconditioned understanding that the *I* contains the world. This is the structure and substance of the elemental *I*, a paradigm actualizing the ability to sincerely experience and express in and from the genuine substance of self. For the Jew, this process is mirrored on a more sophisticated stage as the individual moves first to objectively identify and align with various representative elements of a parent culture and subsequently matures to subjectively unify self with the spiritual substance, or blood, of community. The nationalist Jew may feel great empathic anguish at the suffering of a given Jew or Jewish settlement. The unconditioned Jew – clarified by Buber's distinction between 'religion' and 'religiousness,' where 'religiousness' is the astonished and worshipful feeling of man, that above his conditionality there stands an Unconditioned whose desire is to form a living community with him – owns that suffering as his very own.

In the objective, an individual effectively internalizes environmental constants of language, native geography, peculiarities of culture and normative behavior. He identifies with other individuals who share in these constants of experience and accepts them, in totality, as his people. In this sense, Judaism is a nationality comprised of participating Jews in geographic proximity and Jews otherwise displaced or disaffected, Jews of exile.

In the subjective, the individual moves beyond an identification with external elements of experience and discovers an internalized continuity of communal existence. Buber refers to this inner substance as "blood", the creative force in communal life, communicating through each successive generation the nature and fates of its forebears, their sufferings, deeds and destinies. Where objective and subjective societal and spiritual affiliations are in harmony, the Jew is undivided and actualized, pure and unified.

However, for many Jews, the objective cultural and subjective spiritual substance are in obvious conflict. The more aware and honest the Jew becomes, the more actualized in his inner identification with the Judaic spiritual continuum, the deeper the apparent anguish in reconciling external societal affiliations with the peculiar requirements of the elemental *I*. To further complicate matters, generational participation in the society of exile has necessarily resulted in the assimilation of various, otherwise foreign cultural elements into the innermost forces of the blood. Thus, the Jew in exile is presented with a personal choice which Buber recognizes as the root of all Jewish questions.

The choice is not to embrace either subjective or objective membership at the absolute expense of alternative alignment. Rather, it is a question of supremacy, "what should be dominant and what the dominated (19)." The Jew opting for the dominance of blood is a Jew from within, appropriately assimilating and entirely assimilated into the discrepancies, sufferings and destiny of the Jewish existence. The true interest of the Jew is not a matter of socio-political zeal or creedal endorsement, but of the Jew's absorption into the essence and existence of the Jewish religious reality as manifest in the continuity of blood.

The Jewish unitary tendency is born from an inherent predisposition to perceive phenomena in context, a holistic conceptualization intimating the fullness of a given element or event. This perspective subsequently encourages the Jew to gestalt to a unifying, crowning conceptualization of singular, sustaining truth in the divine. In the descending *Shekinah*, or divine presence, the transcendent divine has become immanent to the experiences and environments of men. The human soul also contains sparks of this divine inclination, the "world-permeating, world-animating, world-being God (43)." The Jew, united with the Judaic religious reality in his inner blood and being, is driven beyond dualism to the unified unconditional as deep calls to deep.

The indwelling *Shekinah*, in man and in all created matter, allows for a deeper examination of the Jewish principle that all acts and initiatives can be undertaken for the sake of the divine in consecration. If all matter contains a spark of the divine inclination, then the use thereof in such a way as reflects the unconditional religious reality of Judaism is, in truth, a restorative recognition of the *dues sive natura*, a consecration of the immanent divine. In such a way, the Jew assists in the destiny of the divine on earth. At the heart of the Jewish eschatological perspective is this yearning for the redemption of the man and matter, the fullness of the indwelling divine. In all things, Buber suggests, the Jew is gifted with greater motor than sensory faculties, demonstrating more of his Jewishness in action than contemplation. Judaism is in the deed.

For this reason, Buber is compelled to draw strong distinctions between Jewish religion and proper Jewish religiosity. In participating in the destiny of the immanent divine, the Jewish deed emanates and acquires an aspect of the infinite. The "fullness of the world's destiny, namelessly interwoven" is manifest in the unconditional act, a unitary communion (86). The truth, then, is not a what but a how. Buber describes this religious reality in writing:

> Jewish religiosity is built neither on doctrine nor on an ethical prescription, but on a fundamental perception that gives meaning

to man: that one thing above all is needed. This perception is transformed into a demand (*Forderung*) wherever religiosity is community-forming and religion-founding, wherever it moves from the life of the individual man into the life of the community (87).

At the heart of that meaning for men is the communion with and adoration of the divine via the eternity of the unconditioned act. Religious law solidifies when the unconditioned divine encounters human self-contradiction, inappropriately casting the indwelling divine inclination in light of the prohibitive and ritualistic. In order to function within the context of community, religiosity does require some consistent, interactive morphology. However, when religion as rite and dogma supercedes the unconditioned adoration of the divine, it ties the Jew to a static statute to the exclusion of individual liberty. When the prophet decries the practice of ritual sacrifice in the utter absence of unconditional adoration, he speaks to the immutable entanglement of a deed divorced from the divine.

Judaism and the Jewish State

Hence Judaism must not liken itself to other nations, for it knows that, being the first-born, realization is incumbent upon it; but neither must it consider itself superior to them, for it has fallen so far short of the ideal image set before it that it is at times barely able to distinguish it. So long, therefore, as the kingdom of God has not come, Judaism will not recognize any man as the true messiah, yet it will never cease to expect redemption to come from man, for it is man's task to establish God's power on earth (111).

The religious reality of Buber's Judaism remains predicated upon the status of contact in relationship to divine revelation. God does not live in the ether, unreachable. Rather, he resides in the unconditioned now, in the space between earthly beings, a core of unity given volition in the actions of the obedient Jew. In service to God, the Jew draws God into life. The Jewish concept of holiness includes ideal and unconditioned community with both God and man. Thus, religion and ethical considerations, nationalist and social principles are unified in the congregational pursuit of holiness, of true human community.

The substance and rhythm of these ideals are reflected in the legal dynamics of the Mosaic state, whereby all debts are to be cancelled and all slaves freed in the seventh year, with a restoration of land ownership to primary titleholder in the fiftieth year. Unlike the Greek polis, which sprawls out upon an infrastructure best characterized by fundamental economic inequality, the initial Jewish State entirely attributes sovereignty, right and resource to the guiding divine. Apparent human leadership constitutes a duly deputized representation of the Divine prerogative. In this pristine estate, the early Israelites remain unfamiliar with the concepts of hereditary leadership and essential class division. It is in this unique identity, now corrupt, that Buber moves to recognize the remnant Israelite spirit preserved into the modern idiom and again gaining voice in the fledgling Israeli state.

The relationship of Jewish individual to Jewish state occurs in the realization and introduction of the unconditioned Jewish *I* into the existential continuity of Jewish blood and history. The Mosaic Commandments are not addressed to the Jewish collective, but to the individual Jewish Thou who participates from essence with the whole of the Jewish identity. Similarly, Jewish culture flourishes only where mutual accomplishment advances from a mutual spirit and life. Buber's aspirations for the modern state of Israel emanate from this interpenetration of spirit and populace. For the Jew, truth must not be an abstraction, ineffectual to the pragmatic political interests of nationalist Zionism. Likewise, the prophetic proclamation of turning remains effective to the execution of the redemptive design relative to the soul, the society and, ultimately, the whole of human civilization.

In order for the Jewish identity to enter into the Jewish state as a realization of its revelatory core, Jewish community must function as an actualization of the divine in the shared life of men. Revolutions fail in their inability to force external, artificial political alternatives into the persistent source of an internally unaffected, shared spiritual existence. Meaningful political change must be predicated upon a fundamental evolution in associated human relationships. Buber is wary of the nationalist overtures which serve as an ideological undercurrent to the Zionist imperative. Nationalism, he observes, has never resulted in genuine renaissance. Rather, true national vitality "has always been based on a passionate reaching out for new human content (140)." True renaissance for an Israelite state requires a foundation of lived religion, its people an "inviolable priest" of the revelation of divine demand.

Judaism and Humanity

Furthermore, the human world is meant to become a single body through the actions of men themselves. We men are charged to perfect our own portion of the universe-the human world. There is one nation that once heard this charge so loudly and clearly that the charge penetrated to the very depths of its soul. That nation accepted the charge, not as an inchoate mass of individuals, but as a nation. As a nation it accepted the truth that calls for its realization by the human nation, the human race as a whole. And that is its spirit, the spirit of Israel (182-3).

Humanity is not without purpose. This purpose is not a matter of human ingenuity or general consensus, does not begin with men, but has been revealed as a prerogative of the guiding divine. The Jewish community then, is its first and most profoundly affected recipient and caretaker, a model congregation rooted in origin and aspect in revelation, in theophany. The charge to reflect, preserve and promote those guiding principles of a religious reality necessary to upright international relations is an essential undercurrent in the continuity of Jewish blood and heritage. Where the eternal Other encounters the whole of humanity, the Jewish identity endures as an apparent artifact and organic evidence of divine design, giving volition to the very destiny of god on earth.

The messianic hope, then, can not be divorced from the necessary obligation of the Jew and Jewish state to participate in the preparations for a coming kingdom of god as presented in the divine demand. Of course, "it is within the power of heaven to introduce the kingdom of god; (but) the preparation of the world in readiness for that kingdom, the beginning of the fulfillment of truth, calls for men and a nation of men (184)." The revelation of the divine demand is a unique event in the history of men. This event is all the more significant when one realizes that it is encoded into the structure and substance of scripture and entrusted to the Jewish community for safe keeping, dependent upon them for preservation and realization in the midst (as a nation) and in the morphology (in exile) of the many, disparate political worlds of men. The Jewish spirit is that of the realization of union, the manifestation of the divine demand.

In this sense, the Jewish faith and function is primarily prophetic, corrective of the errant. God's redemptive design is ever at work in the entirety of human history, leading the evil element into the possibility of reconciliation to truth. The prophetic proclamation, then, is that of an appropriate season of "turning", or finding a direction which is consummated in the unconditioned. Alternative to this perspective is the apocalyptic faith, an unflinching Manichean dualism, which denies the prophetic dynamic of the redemptive principle. Good and evil remain entirely irreconcilable, uncommon and estranged. Where the prophetic faith, the faith of Judaism, sees the possibility of the participation of men in the progressive redemption of creature and creation, the apocalyptic faith denies every possibility of redemptive dialogue between inherently oppositional principles at war in the midst of men.

The Jews move into the international community as a people of Torah, the record of that revelation at the root of the Jewish identity. This adherence to scripture becomes somewhat problematic when one recognizes that a considerable percentage of the gentile world has also appropriated Torah as a pretext to the more apocalyptic conventions of Christian theological doctrine:

> The peoples accepted the gospel, but it came with the Torah of Israel, which comprehends three things: First, the history or creation, which evolves into the history of Israel; second, the revelation of God, which was first of all his revelation to Israel; and third, the Messianic prophecy, whose center and focal point is the effort of the people of Israel for the redemption of humanity (186-7).

The divine demand is comprehensive, a commission towards the proliferation of peace in the pursuit of a greater nation of nations interrelated through realized precepts of justice and righteousness. It "hovers over" the gentile world, an image of the promise and potential of the prophetic proclamation. That is, the strains of creation continue in the redemptive stratagem.

The apparent conflict arises in the apocalyptic utterance of Saul, the presumed "apostle to the gentiles." For the Jew, a messianic ideal evolves from the dissatisfactory experience of state in light of the divine demand. The messianic prophecy, then, is a promise of the sovereign fulfillment of the redemptive strategy set against the obvious failings of human kingship. In the teachings of Saul, this frustration bursts forth into resignation and the realization of a secondary revelation in the incarnate Christ, here identified in the person and work of another Jew, Jesus, through whom the participatory prospects of the divine demand have been both fulfilled and abolished. For the gentile world, a world in which only faith is necessary to registration in redemptive history, the Jew is without history or fulfillment. The Jew then, finds himself in an unfortunate position, standing between the gentile world and its attempt to assimilate the God of Torah in the absence of the Torah's presentation of the divine prerogative for men. It is this position, inherently antagonistic, which Buber cites as the very core of the enduring anti-Semitic sentiment. All other explanation for animosity between Jew and gentile is transitory and superficial.

The subsequent failure does not fall exclusively upon the gentile world. Had the Jewish community successfully met its obligation to evidence the divine demand, it might have moved into relationship with the Christian west as an older brother of sorts. Had the newly renewed Jewish state been able to "drive the plowshare of the normative principle into the hard soil of political fact," it might have earned the right to elevate historical event into the "light of that which is above history." Instead, the pursuit of the powers of those princes to the west has forced deepening rifts into the very substance of Jewish communal life. Of all those dangers facing Judaism as it struggles to a realization of its own intimate and unconditioned identity in light of a divinely ordained role in a comprehensive redemptive demand, the threat of assimilation remains most dire.

The Call to True Community

Where does the world stand? Is the axe laid to the root of the trees-as a Jew on the Jordan once said, rightly and wrongly, that it was in his day- today, at another turn in the ages? And if it is, what is the condition of the roots, themselves? Are they still healthy enough to send sap into the remaining stump and produce a fresh shoot from it? Can the roots be saved? Who can save them? In whose charge are they? Let us recognize ourselves: we are the keepers of the roots. How can we become who we are (201)?

As a people, the Jews have ever endured the call to true community, suffering at various times the myriad ballasts and betrayals of human political constitution. First and most profoundly affected by the realization of the divine demand in revelation, the reborn Jewish state necessarily assumes responsibility for establishing a lead in the redemptive realization of true human community, the congregation of the nations, a personal and political participation in those preparations necessary to preface the promised kingdom of god in the midst of people.

Jewish identity is not an amalgam, does not source to popular productivity or collective interest and initiative. Rather, it is predicated upon the introduction of the unconditioned Jewish *I* into the continuity of Jewish blood, a blood which flows from the revelatory event, the reality of historical theophany. From theophany moves the divine demand, a demand ultimately comprehensive to the whole of humanity. It is in this prophetic possibility that the Jewish community takes form and function, imperfect ambassadors echoing the persistent strains of the dialogue between God and man.

8
Two Types of Faith

Throughout his life, Buber was considerate of the communication of the blessings of salvation to the sinner and restoration to divine favor and to a life in intimate communion with God as realized in the content of the Christian New Testament. His interest in such matters, however, encourages an imperfect theosophical, or religious philosophical dualism relative to the facets of faith, the morphology and substance of belief. On the one hand, faith takes form and function through relationship, predicated upon primary integration of individual or communal identity within the context of religious society. In this case, trust and acceptance flows from intimate proximity to the unconditioned truth. Belief is born of one's identification in existential entirety with the trusted source of truth. This, in Buber's estimation, is the Jewish model of ideal fidelity.

On the other hand, faith finds its face in the relationship of acknowledgment, one's acceptance in existential entirety of truth, itself, promoting progressive personal intimacy with the veritable wellspring. If the truth and trust of faith as state of contact flows naturally from the proximity of subject to object, or vice versa, then faith as relationship of acknowledgment presents truth as catalyst to the perfection of that proximity. As one progressively elects acceptance of the underlying propositions of a perceived truth, one grows nearer to the object of faith.

Key to Buber's characterization of the faith of acknowledgment is its highly specialized or individualistic subtext. The Jew does not elect to become Jewish but rather opens to recognize the reality of his inherent Jewishness. By way of comparison, any genuinely Christian concept of religious relationship must necessarily include the concept of conversion. Acceptance of truth as the initiation of a subject and object relationship presumes a preexistent distance between the two bridged, in part, by human initiative in the crisis of decision, by choice.

Buber is careful not to simplify these two types of faith into antitheticals. Of primary importance in either paradigm is the relationship of object and subject, the nearness to partnership. For the Jew, faith moves from union. For the Christian, faith culminates there.

However, in each instance, the union is the existential epicenter of a religious reality. Thus, true dialogue between these two faiths evolves not between dichotomized dogmatic platforms, but in a joint consideration of the teachings of Christ and the Prophets delivered to men struggling into and stumbling out of genuine relationship with the unconditioned kingdom of God.

The Man of Faith

Both the word of Isaiah and the word of Jesus demand in a similar way, not a faith 'in God', which faith the listeners of both possessed as something innate and as a matter of course, but its realization in the totality of life, and especially when the promise arises from amidst catastrophe, and so particularly points towards the drawing near of God's kingdom. The only difference is that Isaiah looks to it as to a still indefinite future and Jesus as to the present (TF, 29).

As a matter of course, both prophet and Christ find their initial audience either primarily or exclusively among the Jews, for whom simple belief in the existence of God is understood to be unexceptional, a given. However, in each case the subsequent teachings are necessarily corrective in nature. The message, then, is not a matter of belief in abstraction, but a didactic discourse on the appropriate actualization of a fundamental faith manifest in the active (fidelity) and in the receptive (trust).

Faith, then, encompasses those behaviors and beliefs appropriate to the fundamental relationship between the devout and the *dynamis*, the "power in which his being originates (28)." Faith is a process of the actualization of a religious reality, a standing firm, taking place in the realm of relationship.

The prophetic demand for movement from simple belief into an actual relationship characterized by behavioral fidelity, trust and essential stability is often addressed in terms of the correction of perspective, a turning or returning on the part of man or God to fundamental relationship. In the prophetic proclamation, the *teshuvah* (turning of the whole person) constitutes a dialogical principle at play in the corresponding conversation between God and man:

> The call to turn back 'to God' or 'up to God' is the primary word of the prophets of Israel; from it proceed, even when not expressed, promise and curse. The full meaning of this summons is only made known to him who realizes how the demanded

'turning-back' of the people corresponds to God's 'turning-away' from the sphere of His anger or of His 'returning' to Israel (27).

Thus, the turning and returning are not to be understood in terms of suppositional demand and conclusive action. Rather, it is a mutual reaffirmation of fundamental religious relationship, a corrective conversation between the unconditioned *I* and the eternal *Thou*. The danger is in the keeping of the realization of a revealed divine demand in the absence of one's surrender to that demand in the whole of human existence, believing without being, and recitation of rite without appropriate participation in the actual, dialogical faith.

The correction of personal perception in relationship to the unfolding revelation of the divine demand is presented as a necessary precedent to an actualized faith in the teaching and ostensibly divine personage of Jesus, as well. The difference is primarily eschatological in context.

In the preparatory prophetic proclamations of John the Baptist, the New Testament harbinger, the dialogical turning and returning into realized religious relationship is framed in terms of individual turning in light of an appointed hour, now drawing near, culminating in some apparent self-revelation of the coming *Basileia* (kingdom) of God.

The individual must necessarily turn, listen, understand and engage the voice of the Anointed at the appointed time of its self-disclosure. Turning and returning again occur in the narrowing space between man and God, whose kingdom is even now brushing up against the sphere of human experience.

The teachings of Jesus make mention of the kingdom of God in its most intimate of proximities to the realm of men, a nearness which demands existential surrender of self-interest as a prerequisite to meaningful participation. To this end, the storming force of turning in men lays hold of the imminent kingdom.

The turning man "penetrates into the *dynamis*," enters into the universality of potentiality actualized by an absolute surrender of self definition and determination. He does not possess the power of God. Rather, the power of God possesses him. Anything could happen.

Buber isolates three principle messages contained in the teachings of the prophets and of Jesus: Realization of the kingship of God, the necessary turning and returning which constitutes a resumption of the divinely initiated dialogue between God and man, and the ongoing relationship of fidelity and trust which flows from that dialogue. In this much, continuity is preserved between Old and New Testament theosophy. The difference, then, is seen most clearly in the Old

Testament *enumah* (standing firm) and the New Testament *pistis* (faith). Although turning and returning are, at the core, affected in the individual *I*, the Jewish *enumah* is rooted in national Jewish history and ethnic identity. The Christian *pistis*, however, is born in the individual with membership to follow.

The Jewish Messiah

But the prophets never differentiate between the spiritual and the temporal, between the realm of God and the realm of man. For them, the realm of God is nothing more than the realm of man as it is meant to be. Forced to despair of fulfillment in the present, they project the image of their truth into the absolute future; the elaboration of Messianism is the creative expression of this despair (119).

Buber does not accept that the Jewish messianic concept is apocalyptic in origin. It is not meant to be understood in terms of an eschatological framework, not positioned in the end of days, but possessed of a contemporary potentiality, standing in the full reality of the present hour. The messianic era, then, is not a theoretical antithesis to the existing social or spiritual paradigm. Rather, it is a completion of the divine demand realized in the ongoing continuity of human existence. Buber describes it as a detoxified continuation of human history, the purification of the dialogue of days.

As stated in the previous chapter, the prophetic message does not differentiate between spiritual and temporal existence. The "realm of God is nothing more than the realm of man as it was meant to be (119)." As observed, Jewish activism in the interests of the fulfillment of the divine demand, the upward building of peace between nations overseen and administered by the appointed messianic watchman, is vital to the Jewish community's understanding of its own essential identity and its collective responsibility as a holy nation, a unified priesthood bound at the core to the direct revelation of God's design for men. Thus, the messianic revival of Judaism and fulfillment of that divine demand is predicated upon the sincere participation of men in actualized, unconditioned relationship to God.

Through trial and even exile, the idealized messianic kingship develops conceptually as a prophetic alternative to the rather spectacular failure of the Israelite monarchy. Under Roman rule, the messianic perspective finds its normative expression in the priestly congregation of Pharisees. A more radicalized interpretation is unearthed in the self-segregating community of Essenes at Qumran.

Buber notes the indelible influence of both Pharasaical and Essenic thought in framing the teaching and thought of Jesus and the subsequent doctrine of fledgling Christianity.

Buber approaches Essenism as a sectarian expression of the inward pursuit of the participation of determined men in the realization of the messianic prospect. A self-contained and consistent social and economic entity, the Essenic community organized around a sincere regiment of common daily labor, ritualized bathing and the shared ownership and administration of available resource:

Responding to the need and disillusionment of their age, the Essenes begin with realization in their own midst. This does not imply renunciation of hope for the states' transformation; it does signify, however, abandonment of the attempt to achieve such a transformation by words alone. It signifies a desire to build that does not wait for God to make a start but surmises that by building it will become aware of God, its fellow builder. It signifies a will to create the true community by starting where alone a start can be made: here and now (122).

The Essenic community deliberately removed itself from metropolitan life and the affairs of state, forsaking trade for an economic system centered on the bartering of crafts and the gifting of commodities. Although apparently isolationist, the Essenic perspective does not seek to abolish the existing Jewish community, but to build from it an undivided and veritable community capable of planting small seeds of the divine kingdom in the midst of men.

Buber identifies the echoes of this perspective, the desire for human participation in the purification and perfection of Israelite society, as Jesus' most deeply seated Judaism. Thus, when Jesus insists that the subjugated Jewish state must "Render unto Caesar what is Caesar's, and unto God what is God's," there is no implication of any division between world and spirit. To the contrary, Buber writes:

This only appears to be a separation. The state Jesus confronted was no longer a state that one could attempt to recast in its totality by looking its ruler straight in the eye, as the prophet had done with Judea's or Israel's kings; it was not a state that could be conquered by an idea. This was Rome; it was the state pure and simple, which neither knew nor acknowledged anything superior to itself (123-4).

Jesus' confrontation of Rome is not a confrontation of the organism of state, but a confrontation of a legitimized arbitrariness, an unnatural mechanism masquerading as state, an entirely spiritless entity divorced in essence from the very possibility of true human community. The totalitarian rule of man by man is for Jesus, as it was for the Essenes, ultimately godless and unjust.

The appropriate response, then, is not an active resistance of the subjugating state, but a redemptive institution of the legitimate Socio-Spiritual Judaic State against which no worldly alternative can hope to stand. Like the Essenes, Jesus "wished to build the temple of true community out of Judaism, a community whose mere sight would cause the despotic state's walls to crumble" (124). A realized, unified Israel governed by God and undivided in the pursuit of the divine demand would not have to conquer Rome or, by implication, the modern secular state. It would redeem it.

For Jesus, therefore, the interrogative evolves: "How do I get from an apparent life in the revealed word of God to a true life in it, which leads to eternal life" (92)? This question is also a matter of concern to the priestly congregation of Pharisees, whose approach to the issue of essential motivation establishes the seeds of what will become the *lishmah*, the doctrine of the direction of the human heart. Inherently ambivalent, the human heart is without specific volition, swept this way and that by every wind of external agency. What direction might be gained from the world about the *I* is mutable, destabilizing, ultimately serving only to intensify the swirling currents of individual intent. The only true direction of the human heart is that which turns to God. The only true action or interest is that undertaken for the sake of God:

> *Lishmah* means: for the sake of the thing itself. By this word there is expressed first of all the fact that man should learn the torah for its own sake and not because of what it yields; he is to fulfill the commandment for its own sake and not for its advantageous consequences; constantly the note is clearly sounded; for the sake of the teaching, for the sake of the commandment, and thus it is as mentioned comprehensively expressed: All thy works should be done for the sake of God (93).

The outwardness of the divine command has revealed itself within the context of a historical reality preserved within the phenomenon of the Judaic religious reality, a reality codified and outwardly actualized in the commandments within and community without Torah, the law.

78

The law, then, is a consequence of the divine condescension in encounter with the substantively self-contradictory hearts of men, a dynamic dialogue between God and an oftentimes recalcitrant constituency.

For the Pharisee, the answer to the life-problem developing in the midst of man's apparent inability to move towards Torah for the sake of the divine becomes a measure of progressive effort. Man may be incapable of undertaking every interest for the sake of God, but he is capable of learning and practicing the prescriptions of the law. Therefore, men must move to behave for the sake of God and to actualize the law in life if they are to "advance from the 'not for its sake' to the 'for its sake'", to live Torah as human response to the divine dialectic (94).

Like the Pharisee, Jesus is also deeply concerned with the direction of the human heart, oftentimes expressing a critical attitude concerning the "works of the law" or those lawful behaviors which are not sincerely undertaken for the sake of the divine. Jesus, in his Sermon on the Mount, clearly believes the Torah capable of fulfillment not only in the obvious letter of the law, but in the "original intention of its revelation" (79). In the former, he echoes the Pharasaical perspective. In the latter, he moves beyond Sinai and into the "cloud-area of revelation, for only now his words 'but I say unto you' or and 'I say unto you' are opposed to the teachings of the generations" (64).

Jesus speaks as an authentic interpreter of Torah, adequately disclosing the historical revelation of the Word, a disclosure not satisfactorily preserved in Israelite tradition. Therefore, where the Pharisees place the role of *lishmah* in the struggles of men to participate in the redemptive dialogue, Jesus authoritatively inserts a summons to follow himself.

Buber and Pauline Christianity

In the previous chapter, we discussed Buber's differentiation between the principles of prophetic and apocalyptic eschatology. To simplify, the apocalyptic eschatological worldview draws an essential and irreconcilable dichotomy between independent principles of good and evil. The divine demand, then, operates under its own unalterable auspices to an ultimate end: the utter destruction of the ancient enemy.

Men exist in the midst of this conflict, existentially aligned to either interest, though incapable of influencing an inevitable outcome. In comparison, the prophetic perspective places a value on the necessity of human participation in the redemptive ambition of the divine demand, a demand most intimately understood by the Jew. In this much, the prophetic perspective is an essentially social soteriological construct, increasingly actualized among men. In the apocalyptic perspective, Buber identifies a perceived division between the spiritual and secular spheres, a division entirely alien to the Jewish theosophical heart.

As a Jew, Buber understands the teachings of Jewish to be predominantly prophetic in nature, an inspired desire to facilitate human participation in the progressive manifestation of the kingdom of God in the midst of men, beginning with the Jew.

Like the Pharisees, Jesus sees the Torah as being capable of fulfillment in the actual life of the unconditioned Jewish I, understands repentance as a dialogue of the direction of the human heart. Although unmistakably individualistic in emphasis and the assumption of didactic authority, Jesus is, at the core, an unabashed Jew.

That modern Christianity has progressed from the prophetic to the primarily apocalyptic, presuming the possession of the divine initiative in the absence of the cultural content of the divine demand, is presumably the result of the reinterpretation of the teachings of Christ at the hands of another Jew, Saul of Tarsus, the apostle Paul.

Unlike Jesus, Paul refuses to acknowledge Torah as capable of fulfillment in accordance with the aspect of the actual intention of its original revelation. In fact, vital to the foundation of Pauline theosophy is the understanding of Torah as purposefully beyond the very possibility of perfection in the lives of man. Torah, then, exists as an essential indictment of men, serving only to evidence the redemptive necessity of the incarnate Christ, in whom men of faith may partake vicariously of a righteousness well beyond the scope of human potential. Torah calls forth sin in the hearts of men so that it "might abound" and so that men might submit entirely to grace, the freely imparted, unconditioned forgiveness of God.

Paul is determined to place the entire weight of the divine demand upon the unique identity of the incarnate Christ, an identity in which men participate through faith, alone. Works, then, proceed from the relationship of faith as an evidence thereof, a consequence of one's introduction into the Christian religious reality. In and of themselves, however, works are insufficient to establish an individual investment in the self-revelation of the Kingdom of God.

The danger this presents to the prophetic perspective is apparent. If the messianic kingdom is accomplished entirely by grace, in spite of Torah, what are the implications for Jewish communal participation in the realization of the divine demand? Indeed, what of the very substance of Torah, its practical unraveling of divinely ordained standards of behaviors reflective of the visceral revelation of the divine demand within the context of human history?

In Pauline theology, Buber traces the invasion of a Hellenistic dualism, a radical dichotomy of spirit and flesh which inevitably provides ideological justification to the Marcionite school of Gnosticism and associated heresies of the early Christian Church. Buber writes:

> Marcion came to Rome from Asia Minor, bringing with him his own gospel as a kind of spiritual contribution to the destruction of Israel. In his gospel he not only separated the Old Testament from the New Testament and the history of Christianity from the history of Israel, but he also drew a line of demarcation between the deities: On the one side the God of Israel, who is also the creator of this imperfect world and is himself imperfect, being only a just God and not a good God: on the other side the "alien", unknown God who has no concern with this world, yet takes pity on it and redeems it (187).

Thus, the alienation of spirit from flesh, the one glorified and the other demonized, begun in Paul finds its natural expression in the Gnostic perspective, within which Kingdom membership can only be attained through the purely spiritual impartation of *gnosis*, or special knowledge. No value is placed upon the physical universe and no thought given to its place in the redemptive process.

The Church, of course, rejected Marcion, "for it knew that if its traditional link with the creation of the world and the revelation were to be broken, the entire basis of its influence upon the order of this world would be undermined" (188). However, the Christian Church, particularly in its Protestant forms, has continued to struggle in its negotiations between Old and New Testament Scriptures in the light of the spirit and flesh dichotomy at various, historically cyclical junctures. In the meanwhile, the Jews remain a people of Torah, preserving the book and law against the initiatives of a Christian culture that seeks all of the authority of Torah while refusing its accompanying obligations.

What of the Jew?

...We do not today know when the churches will again be faced with the alternative of renunciation, which is an inner death, and external

overthrowal, which is actually the prospect of rebirth out of the darkness of the catacombs.

But this we do know: that the extrusion of the Jewish element from Christianity means an extrusion of the divine demand and concrete Messianism.

But what of us Jews (197)?

As a Jew, Martin Buber approaches Jesus from a sense of substantive fraternity, pursuing those elements and interests in the teachings of Jesus which reveal an unmistakably Jewish identity and understanding. Such elements and interests abound, and in the recorded eyewitness testimony concerning the life and public ministry of Jesus Christ, Buber readily identifies strains of similarity between the Christian Messiah and various Jewish religious sects and standards of the relative idiom. The teachings of Jesus seek to actualize the Jew, to proclaim the force of the turning of the human heart, and to insure the prophetic participation of the Jewish community in the year of the favor of the Lord, that time at which the Kingdom of God has drawn near to the movements of men, revealing limitless possibility, miraculous.

However, Buber finds fewer opportunities for the dialogue between Christian and Jew in the contemporary market of ideas. Modern Christianity is, to be certain, dualist in morphology, drawing radical distinctions between independent principles of good and evil, spirit and flesh, distinctions which deprive the role of the human participant in the divine design of all vitality, all relevance. Remnant Judaism and, even moreso, the Israeli state must be an uncomfortable reminder to the observing Christian of those practical precepts of the Law abandoned to presumption of pervasive grace. This discomfort is the certain stone in the stomach of the anti-Semite, who is confronted by Judaism's preservation of the power of Torah in the midst of men.

Between the two types of faith, that faith which flows from membership and that faith which moves forward from the acceptance of precept, there is still much basis for meaningful dialogue. Each is, after its own paradigm, predicated upon the positioning of man within the context of an ideally unconditioned relationship to the conversant divine, a God who moves to men not as power, but as person. For the Jew, God is the Keeper of a desert people. For the Christian, He is the Healer of the shattered heart. The two are much the same.

9
Eclipse of God

Something is taking place in the depths that as yet needs no name. To-morrow even it may happen that it will be beckoned to from the heights, across the heads of the earthly archons. The eclipse of the light of God is no extinction, even to-morrow that which has stepped in between may give way (EG, 129).

Religion and Reality

This introduction to Buber's life and thought begins and ends with two conversations. The *Overture* concerns a conversation which breaks off prematurely but somehow seems to find a conclusion. The *Epilogue,* on the other hand, concerns a conversation which appears to come to a conclusion but in reality remains inconclusive. In either case, both conversations are deeply concerned with the concept of the character and nature of God.

The relationship between an understanding of a transcendent reality and existential reality is for Buber "the most accurate index of its true character," and the true measure of a particular society's honest evaluation of its progress:

> In some periods, that which men "believe in" as something absolutely independent of themselves is a reality with which they are in a living relation, although they well know that they can form only a most inadequate representation of it. In other periods, on the contrary, this reality is replaced by a varying representation that men "have" and therefore can handle, or by only a residue of the representation, a concept which bears only faint traces of the original image (13).

There is a type of person who understands that any religious belief is simply an intra-psychic projection of fictitious content which the soul misleadingly attributes reality to. Society, according to this particular type of individual, can itself be built upon this idealistic foundation but in the end those in such a society who have "attained to clear knowledge, must recognize that every alleged colloquy with the divine was only a soliloquy, or rather a conversation between various strata of the self (13)."

The Doctrine of Spinoza

Buber engages 17th century Dutch philosopher of religion, Baruch Spinoza (1632-77) in order to illustrate what he believes is a revealing example of substituting a humanistic concept of God for a genuine one. He does this to substantiate the claim that the further the concept of God moves from an explanation of the concrete qualities of humanity the more difficult it is for the individual to grasp both the need for and the possibility of the necessity of a primary *Thou* in daily life.

Buber accuses Spinoza of having "undertaken the greatest anti-anthropomorphic effort ever essayed by the human spirit (15)" in his exploration of the divine attributes of God. By deeming these attributes infinite – Spinoza summarizes the attributes under the headings of "extension" and "thought" – the sum total of all the possible characteristics of God are factored into the abstract ideas of the cosmos and the spirit. Buber writes:

> [Spinoza] failed to avoid this impairment solely because he recognized only the supreme aspect of the relation, but not its core, the dialogue between God and man – the divine voice speaking in what befalls man, and man answering in what he does or forbears to do (17).

Buber does acknowledge, however, that Spinoza was honest in his struggle to come to terms with an intellectual concept of God which would allow the individual to appropriate divine love. The thinking of the present time, unfortunately, is not characterized by such an honest approach. Instead, in trying to lay hold to the idea of the divine as the center of religious concern, it would also attempt to destroy any idea of God which brings the reality of relationship with him in everyday life an impossible task.

Kant's Moral Condition

An argument contrary to that of Spinoza is put forward by Kant, Buber argues: "God is not an external substance, but only a moral condition within us (17)." Kant believed that only a God who was indeed absolute in character could impose upon a creation a code of moral absolutism which they in turn would be inclined to carry out. However, this God for Kant was the practical reason of the individual person and, therefore, the moral absolute was a condition within the person which each person ultimately controlled through right reason. This "categorical imperative" which requires a person to act as if the act were to become universally accepted was for Kant an unfortunate evolution of his skewed perspective on God's character. Buber writes:

> But do we not discover, in the depth of any genuine solitude, that even beyond all social existence – nay, precisely in this realm – there is a conflict between good and evil, between fulfillment and failure to fulfil the purpose embodied in us, in this individual being? And yet I am constitutionally incapable of conceiving of myself as the ultimate source of moral approval or disapproval of myself (18).

It is impossible, Buber believes, to replace the "original source of yes or no" by "any self-encounter (18)."

A Dying God is Dead

According to a Jewish legend, Adam and Eve, when they rejected God on the day of their creation and were driven out of the Garden, saw the sun set for the first time. They were terrified, for they could interpret this phenomenon only as a sign that the world was to sink back into chaos because of their guilt. Both of them wept, sitting face to face, the whole night through, and they underwent a change of heart. Then morning dawned. Adam rose, caught a unicorn, and offered it as a sacrifice in place of himself (24).

Hegel is accused by Buber, and others, of transforming "revealed" religion where God is in fact real and present in reality into "manifest" religion where God becomes manifest in the course of history as a sort of universal spirit representing the progress of history itself. There is no longer anything mysterious about the God of Hegel. He is no longer a personal God who encounters his people or desires to be encountered. For Hegel "individuals are sacrificed and surrendered."

Buber is most critical regarding Hegel's magnification of Kant's God of reason into a radical abstraction and his vanquishing of the existential reality of the *I-Thou* relationship where individual and God meet and commune in and through a reality which is both embodied and beyond the grasp of history.

Nietzche's famous dictum "God is dead," for Buber "dramatically sums up the end situation of the era." He considers the modern philosophers Henri Bergson, (1859-1941), whose ideal of God as the *élan vital* (a basic life force) and Martin Heidegger, (1889-1976), whose idea of God is coupled with being-in-the-world as a part of the individual's own being (his *Dasein*), as two examples of carrying out already established distortions advanced by Kant, Hegel, and Nietzsche.

It is this "eclipse of the light of heaven," the "eclipse of God," which "is the character of the historic hour through which the world is passing (23)." This process of deterioration, however, is not best understood by a chronicle of the downward spiral of man's spirit:

> Man may even do away with the name "god," which after all implies is possessive, and which, if the possessor rejects it, i.e., if ther is no longer a "God of man," has lost its *raison d'etre*: yet He who is denoted by the name lives in the light of His eternity (24).

We are "the slayers," says Buber, and we are the ones who remain dwelling in darkness waiting for death's arrival.

Religion and Philosophy

All meaningful "religiousness," according to Buber, is a revelation that faith in reality moves its possessor toward a living relationship with an absolute Being in a reciprocal and unconditional manner. All meaningful philosophy, on the other hand, consists in turning the practical participation of relationship with an absolute Being into the "cogitative truth" that absolute Being is merely an object from which all other objects are derived.

Philosophy makes the mistake of considering religion as a noetical act, and interprets this act as the knowledge of the essence of religion the knowledge of an object which is beyond actually being known. Faith of this understanding, philosophical faith as it were – unlike the practical faith of religiousness where one believes in the substance of something yet unseen – is an understanding of belief as a concept which has as its object a Being which is never clearly known and, therefore, is not capable of concrete human relation. Buber writes:

Philosophy is grounded on the presupposition that one sees the absolute in universals. In opposition to this, religion, when it has to define itself philosophically, says that it means the covenant of the absolute with the particular, with the concrete (41).

For this very reason alone, Buber argues, the central issue at stake in Christian philosophy, this dispute between the proper application of universals (are they actual things in reality or merely words?), "was in essence a philosophical struggle between religion and philosophy and that is its lasting significance (41)."

Philosophy in Buber's final analysis appears to champion a *ministerial* role in both the coming to proper knowledge of practical faith which compels a person toward intimate and personal relationship with an absolute Being and the actual establishing of this relationship through proper understanding of the connections and differences which exist between infinite and finite beings in process and relationship.

People need knowledge and have a duty to acquire the proper knowledge necessary to punctuate the meaning of their place as individuals in society and to fill up the space of history with the relation to the concrete, to keep the *magisterial* role of faith grounded in an understanding of what is and is not genuine self relating to others and to the mystery of absolute Being.

The differences between the affect of religion and philosophy on a person given the different roles each play is clearly demonstrable, Buber realizes. Both philosophy and religion instinctively move toward a totalization of reality in order to achieve a clear understanding of it. In religion, however, the very being of personhood is thrown into this process of becoming and knowing, whereas in philosophy "even the finger-tips think," – recalling the quote from the *Overture* when Buber writes that a "spiritual person thinks even with the fingertips" – but, unlike the spiritual person, the philosopher's fingertips no longer feel as "thinking overruns and overwhelms all the faculties and provinces of the person (44)."

A Stirring in the Depths

Buber would not necessarily find his philosophy of dialogue at home in a series of monographs designed to introduce the person to the great philosophical thinkers and ideas of history. He would have never characterized himself outright as a philosopher *per se*, not even as a philosopher of religion, unless he was given the forum in which to completely flesh-out his unique understanding of what religious philosophy is really about.

Buber places the relationship between philosophy and religion within the entire history of the progress of the spirit of man as it reaches beyond the natural knowledge which marks the progress of a natural world in time and space and toward an absolute Being-in-relation to itself, an *I* and *Thou* re-union.

The French philosopher Jean-Paul Sartre, (1905-80), wrote of "bad faith." Bad faith is a person viewing himself as either fixed or determined in being or, on the other extreme, imagining himself as one who possesses infinite possibility beyond the natural restrictions of mortality which cannot be transcended in the duration of body and soul. Bad faith would have us become God or abandon God entirely and it is at this critical juncture, Buber would argue, philosophy itself is a sort of bad faith in the very real process of religion's holding fast to God and absolute reality, with its intellectualizing of faith until Being-in-relation becomes Being-in-reflection. He writes:

> The beginning of philosophizing means that this Something – a thing among things, a being among beings, an *It* – changes from an object of imagination, wishes, and feelings to one that is conceptually comprehensible, to an object of thought. If the living quality of the conception of God refuses to enter into this conceptual image, it is tolerated alongside of it, usually in an unprecise form, as in the end identical with it or at least essentially dependent on it. Or it is depreciated as an unsatisfactory surrogate for the help of men incapable of thought (124).

The final stage of this unfortunate development in the process of dehumanization is the most subtle. What will a person place in the room of the spirit left vacant by the instrumental dismantling of faith by reason? Buber believes it is the mastery of the work of the hand guided by the capable and comprehensive network of thought ruling over it as itself an absolute Being-in-relation. The human spirit is eclipsed:

> It may yet imagine that it still remains there as bearer of all things and coiner of all values; in truth, it has also destroyed its own absoluteness along with absoluteness in general. The spirit can now no longer exist as an independent essence. There now exists only a product of human individuals called spirit, a product which they contain and secrete like mucus and urine (125).

There is a process in religious life which is analogous to the philosophical deterioration which occurs in much the same way, Buber writes. In this "pseudoreligious counterpart of the relation of faith," a person in living relation to absolute Being attempts to lift the veil between the hidden mystery of the divine. "I am," says man, "acquainted with the unknown, and I make it known (125)."

The Confession of the Absolute

The subjective knowledge of the one turning-towards, this holding back of an I which does not enter into the action with the rest of the person, an I to which the action is an object – all this dispossesses the moment, takes away its spontaneity. The specifically modern man who has not yet let go of God knows what that means: he who is not present perceives no Presence (126).

What exactly does Buber mean by an "eclipse of God?" We storm the gates of heaven in a futile attempt to turn the mystery of Being-in-relation to the *Thou* into an *It*, an object of knowledge which we can control and manipulate with natural reason energized to take control of the throne of Being-in-the-world. We attempt to relegate Transcendence to a place of irrelevance or illusion.

We believe that with our "being's eye, as with our bodily eye to the sun, and that something can step between our existence and His as between the earth and the sun. That this glance of the being exists, wholly unillusory, yielding no images yet first making possible all images, no other court in the world attests than that of faith (127)."

In our age, Buber believes, the *I-It* relation is the master and ruler of all it surveys. The *I* of this duality is an *I* that seeks to possess all knowledge and create all worlds for its own is an *I* that no longer is able to experience "silence in communication" or a "becoming aware," no longer capable of saying *Thou*. He writes:

This selfhood that has become omnipotent, with all the It around it, can naturally acknowledge God nor any genuine absolute which manifests itself to men as of non-human origin. It steps in between and shuts off from us the light of heaven (129).

The *I-Thou* relationship is eclipsed. But there is always the hope a new epoch might have its start "determined by forces previously invisible or unregarded (129)." The nature of the hour at hand, according to Buber, might appear shut off. But what of the next?

Epilogue

Buber was once a guest of a "noble old thinker" who he had met at a conference where he gave a lecture on adult folks-schools while his companion lectured on elementary folk-schools. United by the word "folk" understood in its broadest definitions, Buber was fascinated with the thinker's radical alterations in his personal *Weltanschauung* just after the war years had past and the horror of man's inhumanity against man had been brought so near to him.

Buber describes the man:

> To be old is a glorious thing when one has not unlearned what it means *to begin*, this old man had even perhaps first learned it thoroughly in old age. He was not at all young, but he was old in a young way, knowing how to begin (EG, 6).

When students of a university in the town where the man lived invited him to lecture there, Buber was pleased to spend a few days in the company of his new friend. "There was a good spirit in his house," he recalls, "the spirit that wills to enter life and does not prescribe to life where it shall let it in (6)."

One morning during his stay, Buber was up early going over proofs of one of his manuscripts; specifically the preface which contained a statement of his personal beliefs. He walked into the study to begin reading and discovered the old man was already at his writing-desk:

> Directly after greeting me he asked me what I had in my hand, and when I told him, he asked whether I would not read it aloud to him. I did so gladly. He listened in a friendly manner but clearly astonished, indeed with growing amazement. When I was through, he spoke hesitatingly, then, carried away by the importance of his subject, ever more passionately (7).

Difficult questions, much like those Buber encountered at another time in his life from the old man with the curious face, begin to pour from this old man's mind:

> How can you bring yourself to say "God" time after time? How can you expect that your readers will take the word in the sense in

which you wish it to be taken? What you mean by the name of God is something above all human grasp and comprehension, but in speaking about it you have lowered it to human conceptualization. What word of human speech is so misused, so defiled, so desecrated as this! All the innocent blood that has been shed for it has robbed it of its radiance. All the injustice that it has been used to cover has effaced its features. When I hear the highest called "God," it seems almost blasphemous (7).

Buber, carefully studying the man and their surroundings, recalls the flaming "kindly clear eyes" and voice of the man as he spoke with passion. When he was finished talking, they both sat silent, facing each other as the room became encircled with "the flowing brightness of early morning." This brightness somehow inspiring his own sense of worldview encouraged Buber to reply with a passion all his own. His thoughts are best represented in their entirety:

Yes, it is the most heavy-laden of all human words. None has become so soiled, so mutilated. Just for this reason I may not abandon it. Generations of men have laid the burden of their anxious lives upon this word and weighed it to the ground; it lies in the dust and bears their whole burden.

The races of man with their religious factions have torn the word to pieces; they have killed for it and died for it, and it bears their finger-marks and their blood. Where might I find a word like it to describe the highest! If I took the purest, most sparkling concept from the inner treasure-chamber of the philosophers, I could only capture thereby an unbinding product of thought. I could not capture the presence of Him whom the generations of men have honored and degraded with their awesome living and dying.

I do indeed mean Him whom the hell-tormented and heaven-storming generations of men mean. Certainly, they draw caricatures and write "God" underneath; they murder one another and say "in God's name." But when all madness and delusion fall to dust, when they stand over against Him in the loneliest darkness and no longer say "He, He" but rather sigh "Thou," shout "Thou," all of them the one word, and when they then add "God," is it not the real God whom they all implore, the One God,

Living God, the God of the children of man? Is it not He who *hears* them?

And just for this reason is not the word "God," the word of appeal, the word which has become a *name*, consecrated in all human tongues for all times? We must esteem those who interdict it because they rebel against the injustice and wrong which are so readily referred to "God" for authorization. But we may not give it up.

How understandable it is that some suggest we should remain silent about the "last things" for a time in order that the misused words may be redeemed! But they are not to be redeemed *thus*. We cannot cleanse the word "God" and we cannot make it whole; but, defiled and mutilated as it is, we can raise it from the ground and set it over an hour of great care (7-8).

When he had finished speaking the early morning brightness had dulled somewhat and the dawn had surrendered to the day. Both men, at the end of their words remained together in the room, considering the exchange of ideas which had just transpired. The old man stood up and walked across the room to Buber, placing a hand on his shoulder and said, "Let us be friends." As abruptly as it had begun, the conversation was over.

Bibliography

Works by Martin Buber

At the Turning: Three Addresses on Judaism (New York: Farrar, Straus, and Young, 1952).

Between Man and Man (New York: Macmillan Company, 1965).

Daniel (New York: McGraw-Hill Company, 1965).

Eclipse of God: Studies in the Relation Between Religion and Philosophy (New York: Harper & Row, 1953).

For the Sake of Heaven (New York: Harper & Row, 1953).

Good and Evil: Two Interpretations (New York: Charles Scribner's Sons, 1952).

Hasidism and the Modern Man (New York: Harper & Row, 1958).

I and Thou (New York: Charles Scribner's Sons).

Israel and Palestine: The History of an Idea (London: East & West Library, 1952).

Israel and the World: Essays in a Time of Crisis (New York: Schocken, 1948).

The Kingship of God (New York: Harper & Row, 1961).

The Knowledge of Man (New York: Harper & Row, 1965).

On Judaism (New York: Schocken, 1967).

The Legend of the Baal-Shem (New York: Harper & Row, 1955).

Mamre: Essays in Religion (Melbourne: Melbourne University Press, 1946).

Moses (Oxford: East & West Library, 1946).

Paths In Utopia (Boston: Beacon Press, 1949).

Pointing the Way: Collected Essays (New York: Harper & Row, 1956).

The Prophetic Faith (New York: Macmillan Company, 1949).

Tales of the Hasidim: The Early Masters (New York: Schocken Books, 1947).

Tales of the Hasidim: The Later Masters (New York: Schocken Books, 1948).

Ten Rungs: Hasidic Sayings (New York: Schocken Books, 1947).

Two Letters to Gandhi. With Judah Magnes and including public letters by Buber and Magnes and the original text of Gandhi's statement about the Jews in Harijan, November 26, 1938.

Two Types of Faith (New York: Harper & Row, 1961).

The Way of Man, According to the Teachings of Hasidism (London: Routledge and Kegan Paul, 1950).

The Way of Response (New York: Schocken Books, 1966).

Works about Martin Buber

Arnett, Ronald C., *Communication and Community: Implications of Martin Buber's Dialogue* (Southern Illinois University Press, 1986).

Cissna, Kenneth N., and Anderson, Rob, *Moments of Meeting: Buber, Rogers, and the Potential for Public Discourse* (State University of New York Press, 2002).

Cohen, Arthur A., *Martin Buber: Studies in Modern European Literature and Thought* (New York: Hillary House, 1957).

Diamond, Malcolm L, *Martin Buber: Jewish Existentialist* (New York: Harper & Row, 1960).

Friedman, Maurice, *Martin Buber's Life and Work*, in three volumes: v.i, *Early years* (1878-1923); v. ii, *Middle Years* (1923-1945); v. iii. *Later Years* (1945-1965), (Detroit: Wayne State University Press, 1988).
----*Martin Buber: The Life of Dialogue* (New York: Harper & Row, 1955).

Friedman, Maurice, and Schilpp, Paul Arthur, Editors, *The Philosophy of Martin Buber,* volume of *The Library of Living Philosophers* (Stuttgart: W. Kohlhammer Verlag, 1962).

Gordon, Hayim, *The Heidegger-Buber Controversy: The Status of the I-Thou* (New York: Greenwood Publishing Company, 2001).

Herberg, Will, *Four Existentialist Theologians* (New York: Doubleday Anchor Books, 1958).

Kepnes, Steven, *The Text as Thou: Martin Buber's Dialogical Hermeneutics and Narrative Theology* (Indiana University Press, 1992).

Martin Buber On Psychology and Psychotherapy: Essays, Letters and Dialogue, editor Judith Buber Agassi (Syracuse University Press, 1999).

Shapira, Avraham, et. al., *Hope for Our Time: Key Trends in the Thought of Martin Buber* (State University of New York Press, 1999).

Silberstein, Laurence J., *Martin Buber's Social and Religious Thought* (New York University Press, 1990).

Trapp, Jacob, *Martin Buber: To Hallow This Life* (New York: Harper & Row, 1958).

Wood, Robert E., *Martin Buber's Ontology: An Analysis of I and Thou* (Northwestern University Press, 1969).

The Writings of Martin Buber, editor, Will Herberg (New York: Meridian Books, 1956).

Chronology

1878	Born Mordecai Martin Buber in Vienna, Austria.
1881	Mother disappears without a trace. Martin sent to Lvov to live with grandfather, Salomon Buber, scholar of the Haskalah, the Jewish Enlightenment.
1892	Returns to live with his father (and his new wife) in Lemberg.
1896	Enters University of Vienna.
1901	Serves as editor of *Die Welt*.
1903	Encounters the work of the Ba'al Shem Tov, (1700-60), the founder of Hasidism.
1906	*Tales of Rabbi Nachman*
1908	*Legend of the Baal Shem*
1909	*Ecstatic Confessions*
1909	Delivers Bar Kochba Lectures in Prague (published in 1911 as *Three Addresses on Judaism*).
(1916- 1924)	Serves as founder and editor of monthly journal, *Der Jude*.
(1923- 1933)	Serves as Professor of Comparative Religion, University of Frankfurt
1923	*Ich und Du (I and Thou)*
1925	Begins German translation of the *Chumas*, the Hebrew Bible, with Franz Rosenzweig (circa 1927).
1938	Flees Nazi Germany for Palestine. Becomes prominent advocate of binational (Arab-Jewish) state.
1945	*For the Sake of Heaven*
1947	*Arab-Jewish Unity*. Testimony before the Anglo-American Inquiry Commission for the Ihud (Union) Association by Judah Magnes and Martin Buber.
1947	*Between Man and Man*
1949	Establishment of the Jewish State in Palestine.
1949	*Paths in Utopia*.
1949	Establishes the School for Adult Educators in Jerusalem.
1950	*Two Types of Faith*
1952	*At the Turning: Three Addresses on Judaism*
1952	*Eclipse of God: Studies in the Relation Between Religion and Philosophy*
1952	*Israel and Palestine: The History of an Idea*
1953	*Good and Evil: Two Interpretations*
1958	Martin's wife, Paula Buber dies.
1965	Dies at Home in Jerusalem. Buried in the cemetery Har-Hamenuchot in Jerusalem.